WALKING ON WATER
REFLECTIONS ON FAITH AND ART

COMMEMORATIVE EDITION

IN HONOR OF MADELEINE L'ENGLE'S
80TH BIRTHDAY

MADELEINE L'ENGLE

WALKING ON WATER

REFLECTIONS ON FAITH AND ART

COMMEMORATIVE EDITION

Harold Shaw Publishers
Wheaton, Illinois

Grateful acknowledgment is made to Farrar, Straus and Giroux, Inc. for permission to include an excerpt from A CIRCLE OF QUIET by Madeleine L'Engle. Copyright © 1972 by Madeleine L'Engle Franklin. Reprinted by permission of Farrar, Straus and Giroux, Inc.

ISBN 0-87788-896-5
(Formerly published under ISBN 0-87788-919-8)

Cover design by David LaPlaca

Library of Congress Cataloging-in-Publication Data

L'Engle, Madeleine.
Walking on water.
    1. Christianity and the arts.2. L'Engle,
    Madeleine. I. Title.
    BR115.A8L A6 801'.980-21066
    ISBN 0-87788-896-5

Printed in the United States of America

05 04 03 02 01 99

21 20 19 18 17 16 15

for Bion and
Laurie

CONTENTS

CHAPTER ONE

COSMOS FROM CHAOS

The apple trees in the orchard at Crosswicks are growing old. Last winter the beautiful green pie-apple tree died during the ice storms. This summer I notice that the leafing of some of the others is thin. A neighboring farmer friend tells me that these trees have been "winter killed."

When the children were little we used to tie presents, presents and balloons, on the trees for summer birthdays. This year the willow by the north meadow was hung with balloons and a big basket of blooming ivy-geraniums as we prepared for a spring wedding. A lot of water has run under the stone bridge of the brook since the birthday trees. The pebbly shoreline of Dog Pond, where the children learned to swim, has been tarred for motorboat launching, so that the utter stillness of the lake is often broken. But there is still a pattern to the summers which I hope will never change, a lovely kaleidoscope of family and friends coming and going. Quite a few of the photographs taken at the time of this spring's wedding show me in a typical position, standing at the stove, stirring something. In the summer I seem to spend my days between the stove and the typewriter, with time out for walking the dogs to the brook, bearing the big red clippers which help to clear the paths.

I sit on my favourite rock, looking over the brook, to take time away from busyness, time to *be*. I've long since stopped feeling guilty about taking *being* time; it's something we all need for our spiritual health, and often we don't take enough of it.

This spring I was given two posters which I find helpful in reminding me to take *being* time. (Both givers must have known I needed the message.) A few weeks before the wedding I ran impetuously out to the dark garage to turn on the outside light and rammed into a cardboard cat carrier—mere cardboard, mind you!—and broke the third metatarsal bone in my foot. I have frequently taken mammoth, crashing tumbles without breaking a bone. What a way to do it now! Humiliating, to say the least, and my children rub it in by emphasizing the *cardboard*.

"Can you stay off your feet for six weeks?" the doctor asked.

"No, I'm off day after tomorrow for a ten-day lecture tour all over Ohio. Then we have the wedding, and then I get my grandchildren for a week. . . ."

So off I went, leg in cast, via wheelchair and crutches and elegant pre-boarding on planes. The first poster was given me on my second stop, the

Convent of the Transfiguration near Cincinnati, where I was conducting a retreat. The poster tells me: *Listen to the silence. Stay open to the voice of the Spirit.*

The second poster came a month later, when I was out of the cast but still on crutches, sent me by Luci Shaw, who is largely responsible for my struggling to write this book. It shows a covered bridge in the autumn, very much like the covered bridge we drive through en route to Crosswicks, and it echoes my need: *Slow me down, Lord.*

Good messages. When I am constantly running there is no time for being. When there is no time for being there is no time for listening. I will never understand the silent dying of the green pie-apple tree if I do not slow down and listen to what the Spirit is telling me, telling me of the death of trees, the death of planets, of people, and what all these deaths mean in the light of love of the Creator, who brought them all into being, who brought me into being, and you.

This questioning of the meaning of being, and dying and being, is behind the telling of stories around tribal fires at night; behind the drawing of animals on the walls of caves; the singing of melodies of love in spring, and of the death of green in autumn. It is part of the deepest longing of the human psyche, a recurrent ache in the hearts of all of God's creatures.

So when the two messages, *Listen to the silence. Stay open to the voice of the Spirit,* and *Slow me down, Lord,* came, I was forced to listen, and even to smile as I heard myself saying emphatically to Luci, "No, I most certainly *do not* want to write about being a Christian artist," for I realized that the very vehemence of my reaction meant that perhaps I should, in fact, stop and listen. The Holy Spirit does not hesitate to use any method at hand to make a point to us reluctant creatures.

Why is it that I, who have spent my life writing, struggling to be a better artist, and struggling also to be a better Christian, should feel rebellious when I am called *a Christian artist?* Why should I feel reluctant to think or write about Christian creativity?

It's more than just that I feel the presumption of someone like me, wife, grandmother, storyteller, attempting such a task. I wouldn't even consider it had I not already struggled with it in talks which Mel Lorentzen, Bea Batson, and others in the English department at Wheaton College have pulled out of me. It was some of these faltering lectures which caused Luci and Harold Shaw to ask me to expand my thoughts into a book. And then came Ayia Napa.

Probably it was Ayia Napa that clinched it. When Dr. Marion van Horne asked me to come to Ayia Napa, in Cyprus, for two weeks, how could I resist? I love to travel. My brief trip several years ago to Greece and the Greek islands made me love the incredible blue and gold air of this land where Apollo drove his chariot across the sky, where John brought the mother of Jesus, where Pythagorus walked on the beach, and where Paul preached a message of love even more brilliant than the sun.

Who could resist a trip to Cyprus? To teach at a conference on literature and literacy for delegates from twenty-two underdeveloped and developing countries all over the world, delegates whose only common denominator was Christianity—every denomination and brand and variety of Christianity. And what was I being asked to lecture about? The Christian artist.

Christian art? Art is art, painting is painting; music is music; a story is a story. If it's bad art, it's bad religion, no matter how pious the subject. If it's good art—and there the questions start coming, questions which it would be simpler to evade.

In college I read some aesthetics: Plato, Aristotle; a great chronological jump to Lamb, Coleridge, Wordsworth, Pater, Ruskin. Plato spoke of the necessity for divine madness in the poet. It is a frightening thing to open oneself to this strange and dark side of the divine; it means letting go of our sane self-control, that control which gives us the illusion of safety. But safety is only an illusion, and letting it go is part of listening to the silence, and to the Spirit.

Plato also wrote—and I lettered this in firm italic letters and posted it on my dorm-room door—*All learning which is acquired under compulsion has no hold upon the mind.*

I'm not sure he was right there. During my school and college years I learned a good bit under at least moderate compulsion. I'd never have taken math or science had they been optional (but I enjoyed the poster on my dormitory door!).

What I remember from Ruskin is the phrase: *the cursed animosity of inanimate objects,* which I mutter under my breath when I get in a tangle of wire coat hangers. I also wonder if there *is* any such thing as an inanimate object.

From Coleridge comes the phrase *the willing suspension of disbelief,* that ability to believe which is born firmly in all children, and which too often withers as we are taught that the world of faerie and imagination is not true.

Aristotle reinforces Coleridge when he writes, *That which is impossible and probable is better than that which is possible and improbable.*

Not long after I was out of college I read Leo Tolstoy's *What Is Art?* and I approached it with reverence and hope. Surely this great writer would provide me with the definitive definition, would show me all the answers. He didn't, and I was naive to expect him to. Generally what is more important than getting watertight answers is learning to ask the right questions.

What do they have in common, all these people I read in college and thereafter? All men, and all dead. Their distance from us in chronology seems to give them overwhelming authority. But they were not dead when they wrote, and they were as human as the rest of us. They caught colds in damp weather and had occasional pimples in adolescence. I like to think that they enjoyed making love, spending an evening with friends, tramping through the woods with the dogs. The fact that they were men simply speaks for their day when women may have been powers behind the throne, but they were kept behind it.

Whatever possessed these writers to sit down and write their views on the creative process? Maybe they were prodded, as I have been, and maybe at least a few of them hesitated at the presumption of it.

All right. So it's an impossible task. But thinking about it may open new questions, new insights. And as I listen to the silence, I learn that my feelings about art and my feelings about the Creator of the Universe are inseparable. To try to talk about art and about Christianity is for me one and the same thing, and it means attempting to share the meaning of my life, what gives it, for me, its tragedy and its glory. It is what makes me respond to the death of an apple tree, the birth of a puppy, northern lights shaking the sky, by writing stories.

Recently I picked up a *New Yorker* on a plane trip and saw a cartoon of two men at a bar, one a great muscular hulk of a man, and the other half his size, scrawny and ineffectual looking. And the small man is saying, " . . . but I repeat, this is only my very, very, humble, humble opinion." Just so, I offer my very, very, humble, humble opinion on the vast topic of the Christian and art.

I go to the dictionary, and it isn't much help. Both *Webster's Collegiate* and the *Concise Oxford* report that a Christian is a person believing in the religion of Christ. As for art, in both these dictionaries it is limited to skill, as "skill, especially human skill as opposed to nature; skill applied to imitation and design, as in painting, etc.; a thing in which skill may be exercised; those in which mind and imagination are chiefly concerned."

Skill may be learned, and if art is merely a skill, then it can be acquired by anybody, and being a painter would merely be the equivalent of being a good dentist's technician or a practiced butcher.

It is an honorable thing to be a dentist's technician or a butcher, but neither would claim to be a creator.

Leonard Bernstein tells me more than the dictionary when he says that for him music is *cosmos in chaos.* That has the ring of truth in my ears and sparks my creative imagination. And it is true not only of music; all art is cosmos, cosmos found within chaos. At least all Christian art (by which I mean all true art, and I'll go deeper into this later) is cosmos in chaos. There's some modern art, in all disciplines, which is not; some artists look at the world around them and see chaos, and instead of discovering cosmos, they reproduce chaos, on canvas, in music, in words. As far as I can see, the reproduction of chaos is neither art, nor is it Christian.

e. e. cummings lauds the beauty of cosmos as he sings,

i who have died am alive again today,
and this is the sun's birthday, this is the birth
day of life and love and wings; and of the gay
great happening illimitably earth

      . . .

now the ears of my ears are awake and
now the eyes of my eyes are opened

And the psalmist sings, "O taste and see how gracious The Lord is: blessed is the man who trusteth in him" and "The heavens declare the glory of God: and the firmament showeth his handiwork. . . ."

And I rejoice. But I have no idea what "denomination" or "brand" of faith cummings professed, if any, and the psalmist who wrote those lines died long before the birth of Jesus in Bethlehem. So perhaps the reason I shuddered at the idea of writing something about "Christian art" is that to paint a picture or to write a story or to compose a song is an incarnational activity. The artist is a servant who is willing to be a birth-giver. In a very real sense the artist (male or female) should be like Mary, who, when the angel told her that she was to bear the Messiah, was obedient to the command.

Obedience is an unpopular word nowadays, but the artist must be obedient to the work, whether it be a symphony, a painting, or a story for a small child. I believe that each work of art, whether it is a work of great genius or something very small, comes to the artist and says, "Here I am. Enflesh me. Give birth to me." And the artist either says, "My soul doth magnify the Lord," and willingly becomes the bearer of the work, or refuses; but the obedient response is not necessarily a conscious one, and not everyone has the humble, courageous obedience of Mary.

As for Mary, she was little more than a child when the angel came to her; she had not lost her child's creative acceptance of the realities moving on the other side of the everyday world. We lose our ability to see angels as we grow older, and that is a tragic loss.

God, through the angel Gabriel, called on Mary to do what, in the world's eyes, is impossible, and instead of saying, "I can't," she replied immediately, "Be it unto me according to thy word."

God is always calling on us to do the impossible. It helps me to remember that anything Jesus did during his life here on earth is something we should be able to do, too.

When spring-fed Dog Pond warms up enough for swimming, which usually isn't until June, I often go there in the late afternoon. Sometimes I will sit on a sun-warmed rock to dry, and think of Peter walking across the water to meet Jesus. As long as he didn't remember that we human beings have forgotten how to walk on water, he was able to do it.

If Jesus of Nazareth was God become truly man for us, as I believe he was, then we should be able to walk on water, to heal the sick, even to accept the Father's answer to our prayers when it is not the answer that we hope for, when it is *no*. Jesus begged in anguish that he be spared the bitter cup and then humbly added, "but not as I will, Father; as you will."

In art, either as creators or as participators, we are helped to remember some of the glorious things we have forgotten, and some of the terrible things we are asked to endure, we who are children of God by adoption and grace.

In one of his dialogues, Plato talks of all learning as remembering. The chief job of the teacher is to help us to remember all that we have forgotten.

This fits in well with Jung's concept of racial memory, his belief that when we are enabled to dip into the intuitive, subconscious self, we remember more than we know. One of the great sorrows which came to human beings when Adam and Eve left the Garden was the loss of memory, memory of all that God's children are meant to be.

Perhaps one day I will remember how to walk across Dog Pond.

At Ayia Napa I talked about the artist as birth-giver, as one still able to see angels, and after the lecture there was considerable buzzing among some of these young Christian delegates. "Does she really think she can see angels?" "What's all this about angels?"

It turned out that their idea of angels came from illustrations in children's books, *Christian* children's books, rather than from reading about them in the Bible. It is impossible to read the Bible regularly and carefully and not pay attention to angels. It is probably because we lose our ability to see angels as we grow up that the grown-up artist's depiction of angels is so unbelievable.

Recently I received a letter from a perspicacious eleven-year-old: "As I read the descriptions of the cherubim, Progo, in *A Wind in the Door,* it seems to me that you are describing him like the cherubims in the Bible. Did you do this on purpose?"

Yes, of course.

Cherubim, seraphim, all the angelic host as they are described in Scripture, have a wild and radiant power that often takes us by surprise. They are not always gentle. They bar the entrance to Eden so that we may never return home. They send plagues upon the Egyptians. They are messengers of God. They are winds. They are flames of fire. They are young men dressed in white.

Three of them come to Abraham to be his guests. One wrestles all night long with Jacob. They minister to Jesus after the temptations in the wilderness. They are God come to tell us something, and in the Old Testament it is obvious that God's people understand that angels are voices and appearances of the Master of the Universe himself. To be visited by an angel is to be visited by God. To be touched by an angel is to be touched by God, and it is a terrifying experience. When the angel smote him on the thigh, Jacob limped forever after. Daniel, who had braved lions, trembled and fainted at the appearance of the Lord's angel. And John, on the Isle of Patmos, fell down as though dead.

We talked a lot about angels that day at Ayia Napa, angels as they appear in the Bible, and quite a few misapprehensions were cleared up. When they really examined themselves, most of the delegates found out that they did, after all, believe in angels.

I believe in angels; guardian angels; the angel who came to Gideon and told a shy, not very brave young man that he was a man of valour who was going to free his people; the angels who came to Jesus in the agony of the garden. And, what is less comforting, avenging angels, destroying angels, angels who come bringing terror when any part of God's creation becomes too rebellious, too full of pride to remember that they are God's creatures.

And, most fearful of all, fallen angels, angels who have left God and followed Lucifer and daily offer us their seductive and reasonable temptations. If we read the Bible, and if what we read has anything to do with what we believe, then we have no choice but to take angels seriously; and most artists do, from Milton to Doré to Shakespeare to . . .

The artist, if he is not to forget how to listen, must retain the vision which includes angels and dragons and unicorns and all the lovely creatures which our world would put in a box marked *Children Only*.

How difficult we find the Annunciation (angels again!). And how could one young, untried girl contain within her womb the power which created the galaxies? How could that power be found in the helplessness of an infant? It is more than we, in our limited, literal-mindedness, can cope with, and so we hear, "I can't be a Christian because I can't believe in the virgin birth," as though faith were something which lay within the realm of verification. If it can be verified, we don't need faith.

I don't need faith to know that if a poem has fourteen lines, a specific rhyme scheme, and is in iambic pentameter, it is a sonnet; it may not be a good sonnet, but it will be a sonnet. I don't need faith to know that if I take flour and butter and milk and seasonings and heat them in a double boiler, the mix will thicken and become white sauce. Faith is for that which lies on the *other* side of reason. Faith is what makes life bearable, with all its tragedies and ambiguities and sudden, startling joys. Surely it wasn't reasonable of the Lord of the Universe to come and walk this earth with us and love us enough to die for us and then show us everlasting life? We will all grow old, and sooner or later we will die, like the old trees in the orchard. But we have been promised that this is not the end. We have been promised life.

What would have happened to Mary (and to all the rest of us) if she had said *no* to the angel? She was free to do so. But she said *yes*. She was obedient, and the artist, too, must be obedient to the command of the work, knowing that this involves long hours of research, of throwing out a month's work, of going back to the beginning, or, sometimes, scrapping the whole thing. The artist, like Mary, is free to say *no*. When a shoddy novel is published the writer is rejecting the obedient response, taking the easy way out. But when the words mean even more than the writer knew they meant, then the writer has been listening. And sometimes when we listen, we are led into places we do not expect, into adventures we do not always understand.

Mary did not always understand. But one does not have to understand to be obedient. Instead of understanding—that intellectual understanding which we are so fond of—there is a feeling of rightness, of knowing, knowing things which we are not yet able to understand.

During the question-and-answer period after a lecture, a young woman said to me, "I read *A Wrinkle in Time* when I was eight or nine. I didn't understand it, but I knew what it was about."

As long as we know what it's about, then we can have the courage to go wherever we are asked to go, even if we fear that the road may take us through danger and pain.

If the work comes to the artist and says, "Here I am, serve me," then the job of the artist, great or small, is to serve. The amount of the artist's talent is not what it is about. Jean Rhys said to an interviewer in the *Paris Review*, "Listen to me. All of writing is a huge lake. There are great rivers that feed the lake, like Tolstoy and Dostoyevsky. And there are mere trickles, like Jean Rhys. All that matters is feeding the lake. I don't matter. The lake matters. You must keep feeding the lake."

To feed the lake is to serve, to be a servant. *Servant* is another unpopular word, a word we have derided by denigrating servants and service. To serve should be a privilege, and it is to our shame that we tend to think of it as a burden, something to do if you're not fit for anything better or higher.

I have never served a work as it ought to be served; my little trickle adds hardly a drop of water to the lake, and yet it doesn't matter; there is no trickle too small. Over the years I have come to recognize that the work often knows more than I do. And with each book I start, I have hopes that I may be helped to serve it a little more fully. The great artists, the rivers and tributaries, collaborate with the work, but for most of us, it is our greatest privilege to be its servant.

When the artist is truly the servant of the work, the work is better than the artist; Shakespeare knew how to listen to his work, and so he often wrote better than he could write; Bach composed more deeply, more truly, than he knew; Rembrandt's brush put more of the human spirit on canvas than Rembrandt could comprehend.

When the work takes over, then the artist is enabled to get out of the way, not to interfere. When the work takes over, then the artist listens.

But before he can listen, paradoxically, he must work. Getting out of the way and listening is not something that comes easily, either in art or in prayer.

Before I can listen to God in prayer, I must fumble through the prayers of words, of willful demands, the prayers of childish "Gimmes," of "Help mes," of "I want. . . ." Until I tell God what I want, I have no way of knowing whether or not I truly want it. Unless I ask God for something, I do not know whether or not it is something for which I ought to ask, and I cannot add, "But if this is not your will for me, then your will is what I want, not mine." The prayers of words cannot be eliminated. And I must pray them daily, whether I feel like praying or not. Otherwise, when God has something to say to me, I will not know how to listen. Until I have worked through self, I will not be enabled to get out of the way.

Someone wrote, "The principal part of faith is patience," and this applies, too, to art of all disciplines. We must work every day, whether we feel like it or not; otherwise when it comes time to get out of the way and listen to the work, we will not be able to heed it.

CHAPTER TWO

ICONS OF THE TRUE

It has often struck me with awe that some of the most deeply religious people I know have been, on the surface, atheists. Atheism is a peculiar state of mind; you cannot deny the existence of that which does not exist. I cannot say, "That chair is not there," if there is no chair there to say it about.

Many atheists deny God because they care so passionately about a caring and personal God and the world around them is inconsistent with a God of love, they feel, and so they say, "There is no God." But even denying God, to serve music, or painting, or words is a religious activity, whether or not the conscious mind is willing to accept that fact. Basically there can be no categories such as "religious" art and "secular" art because all true art is incarnational, and therefore "religious."

The problem of pain, of war and the horror of

war, of poverty and disease is always confronting us. But a God who allows no pain, no grief, also allows no choice. There is little unfairness in a colony of ants, but there is also little freedom. We human beings have been given the terrible gift of free will, and this ability to make choices, to help write our own story, is what makes us human, even when we make the wrong choices, abusing our freedom and the freedom of others. The weary and war-torn world around us bears witness to the wrongness of many of our choices. But lest I stumble into despair I remember, too, seeing the white, pinched-faced little children coming to the pediatric floor of a city hospital for open-heart surgery and seeing them two days later with colour in their cheeks, while the nurses tried to slow down their wheelchair races. I remember, too, that there is now a preventative for trachoma, still the chief cause of blindness in the world. And I remember that today few mothers die in childbirth, and our graveyards no longer contain the mute witness of five little stones in a row, five children of one family, dead in a week of scarlet fever or diptheria.

George MacDonald gives me renewed strength during times of trouble—times when I have seen people tempted to deny God—when he says, "The Son of God suffered unto death, not that men might not suffer, but that their sufferings might be like his."

Jesus, too, had to make choices, and in the eyes of the world some of his choices were not only contrary to acceptable behaviour, but were foolish in the extreme. He bucked authority by healing on the Sabbath; when he turned his steps towards Jerusalem he was making a choice which led him to Calvary.

It is the ability to choose which makes us human.

This ability, this necessity to choose, is an important element in all story. Which direction will the young man take when he comes to the crossroads? Will the girl talk with the handsome stranger? Should the child open the forbidden door?

Oedipus killed the man he met at the crossroads, and even though he did not know that the man was his father, that did not allow him to escape the retribution which followed his choice. He married a woman he did not know to be his mother, but his lack of knowledge did not make him innocent. Though we may cry out, "But I didn't know!" our anguish does little to forestall the consequences of our actions. To the nonbeliever, the person who sees no cosmos in chaos, we are all the victims of the darkness which surrounds our choices; we have lost our way; we do not know what is right and what is wrong; we cannot tell our left hand from our right. There *is* no meaning.

But to serve any discipline of art, be it to chip a David out of an unwieldy piece of marble, to take oils and put a clown on canvas, to write a drama about a young man who kills his father and marries his mother and suffers for these actions, to hear a melody and set the notes down for a string quartet, is to affirm meaning, despite all the ambiguities and tragedies and misunderstanding which surround us.

Aeschylus writes, "In our sleep, pain that cannot forget falls drop by drop upon the heart and in our own despair, against our will, comes wisdom through the awful grace of God."

We see that wisdom and that awful grace in the silence of the Pièta, in Gerard Manley Hopkins's poems; in Poulenc's organ concerto, but we do not find it in many places where we would naturally expect to find it. This confusion comes about because much so-called religious art is in fact bad art, and therefore bad religion. Those angels rendered by grown-ups who obviously didn't believe in angels and which confused the delegates at Ayia Napa are only one example. Some of those soppy pictures of Jesus, looking like a tubercular, fair-haired, blue-eyed goy, are far more secular than a Picasso mother and child. The Lord Jesus who rules my life is not a sentimental, self-pitying weakling. He was a Jew, a carpenter, and strong. He took into his own heart, for our sakes, that pain which brings "wisdom through the awful grace of God."

It is impossible for an artist to attempt a graphic reproduction of Jesus in any way that is meant to be literal. I sympathize with the Hassidic teaching that it is wrong to try in any way to make pictures of God or his prophets. The Muslims have this philosophy, too, hence the intricate, nonrepresentational designs on the mosques.

But in a way both miss the point which the Eastern Orthodox artists are taught when they study the painting of icons. The figure on the icon is not meant to represent literally what Peter or John or any of the apostles looked like, nor what Mary looked like, nor the child, Jesus. But, the orthodox painter feels, Jesus of Nazareth did not walk around Galilee faceless. The icon of Jesus may not look like the man Jesus two thousand years ago, but it represents some *quality* of Jesus, or his mother, or his followers, and so becomes an open window through which we can be given a new glimpse of the love of God. Icons are painted with firm discipline, much prayer, and anonymity. In this way the iconographer is enabled to get out of the way, to listen, to serve the work.

An icon is a symbol, rather than a sign. A sign may point the way to something, such as: *Athens— 10 kilometers*. But the sign is not Athens, even when we reach the city limits and read *Athens*. A symbol, however, unlike a sign, contains within it some quality of what it represents. An icon of the Annunciation, for instance, does more than point to the angel and the girl; it contains, for us, some of Mary's acceptance and obedience, and so affects our own ability to accept, to obey.

Francis of Assisi says that "in pictures of God and the blessed Virgin painted on wood, God and the blessed Virgin are held in mind, yet the wood and the painting ascribe nothing to themselves, because they are just wood and paint; so the servant of God is a kind of painting, that is, a creature of God in which God is honoured for the sake of his benefits. But he ought to ascribe nothing to himself, just like the wood or the painting, but should render honour and glory to God alone."

I travel with a small icon, a picture pasted on wood, which was given to me with love, so that the picture, the wood, and the love have become for me a Trinity, an icon of God. Of themselves they are nothing; because they are also part of God's munificent love they are everything.

(A parenthesis here about quotations and credits. I was taught in college how to footnote, how to give credit where credit is due, and in the accepted, scholarly way. But most of the writers I want to quote in this book are writers whose words I've copied down in a big, brown, Mexican notebook, what is called a commonplace book. I copy down words and thoughts upon which I want to meditate, and footnoting is not my purpose; this is a devotional, not a scholarly notebook. I've been keeping it for many years, and turn to it for help in prayer, in understanding. All I'm looking for in it is meaning, meaning which will help me to live life lovingly, and I am only now beginning to see the usefulness of noting book title and page, rather than simply jotting down, "Francis of Assisi.")

An iconographer is a devout and practicing Christian, but all true art has an iconic quality. An Eastern Orthodox theologian, Timothy Kallistos Ware, writes (and where? in a magazine called *Sobornost,* probably about a decade ago, edited by the Rev. Canon A. M. Allchin, of Canterbury Cathedral, England) that

> an abstract composition by Kandinsky or Van Gogh's landscape of the cornfield with birds . . . is a real instance of divine transfiguration, in which we see matter rendered spiritual and entering into the "glorious liberty of the children of God." This remains true, even when the artist does not personally believe in God. Provided he is an artist of integrity, he is a genuine servant of

the glory which he does not recognize, and unknown to himself there is "something divine" about his work. We may rest confident that at the last judgment the angels will produce his works of art as testimony on his behalf.

(Angels again!)

We may not like that, but we call the work of such artists un-Christian or non-Christian at our own peril. Christ has always worked in ways which have seemed peculiar to many men, even his closest followers. Frequently the disciples failed to understand him. So we need not feel that we have to understand how he works through artists who do not consciously recognize him. Neither should our lack of understanding cause us to assume that he cannot be present in their work.

A sad fact which nevertheless needs to be faced is that a deeply committed Christian who wants to write stories or paint pictures or compose music to the glory of God simply may not have been given the talent, the gift, which a non-Christian, or even an atheist, may have in abundance. God is no respecter of persons, and this is something we are reluctant to face.

We would like God's ways to be like our ways, his judgments to be like our judgments. It is hard for us to understand that he lavishly gives enormous talents to people we would consider unworthy, that he chooses his artists with as calm a disregard of surface moral qualifications as he chooses his saints.

Often we forget that he has a special gift for each one of us, because we tend to weigh and measure such gifts with the coin of the world's marketplace. The widow's mite was worth more than all the rich men's gold because it represented the focus of her life. Her poverty was rich because all she had belonged to the living Lord. Some unheard-of Elizabethan woman who led a life of selfless love may well be brought before the throne of God ahead of Shakespeare, for such a person may be a greater force for good than someone on whom God's blessings seem to have been dropped more generously. As Emmanuel, Cardinal Suhard says, "To be a witness does not consist in engaging in propaganda, nor even in stirring people up, but in being a living mystery. It means to live in such a way that one's life would not make sense if God did not exist."

The widow's mite and Bach's St. Matthew's Passion are both "living mysteries," both witness to lives which affirm the loving presence of God.

Kandinsky and van Gogh say more than they know in their paintings. So does a devout man who is not a Christian but a Jew and a philosopher, Martin Buber. Listen: "You should utter words as though heaven were opened within them and as though you did not put the word into your mouth, but as though you had entered the word." Buber was certainly not consciously thinking of the second Person of the Trinity when he wrote that. Nevertheless his words become richer for me when I set them alongside these: "In the beginning was the Word, and the Word was with God, and the Word was God."

Plato, too, all that distance away in time and space from Bethlehem, seems often to be struggling towards an understanding of incarnation, of God's revelation of himself through particularity. Of course, because I am a struggling Christian, it's inevitable that I superimpose my awareness of all that happened in the life of Jesus upon what I'm reading, upon Buber, upon Plato, upon the book of Daniel. But I'm not sure that's a bad thing. To be truly Christian means to see Christ everywhere, to know him as all in all.

I don't mean to water down my Christianity into a vague kind of universalism, with Buddha and Mohammed all being more or less equal to Jesus—not at all! But neither do I want to tell God (or my friends) where he can and cannot be seen. We human beings far too often tend to codify God, to feel that we know where he is and where he is not, and this arrogance leads to such things as the Spanish Inquisition and the Salem witch burnings and has the result of further fragmenting an already broken Christendom.

We live by revelation, as Christians, as artists, which means that we must be careful never to get set into rigid molds. The minute we begin to think we know all the answers, we forget the questions, and we become smug like the Pharisee who listed all his considerable virtues and thanked God that he was not like other men.

Unamuno might be describing the artist as well as the Christian as he writes, "Those who believe they believe in God, but without passion in the heart, without anguish of mind, without uncertainty, without doubt, and even at times without despair, believe only in the idea of God, and not in God himself."

When I was in college I knew that I wanted to be a writer. And to be a writer means, as everyone knows, to be published.

And I copied in my journal from Tchekov's letters: "You must once and for all give up being worried about successes and failures. Don't let that concern you. It's your duty to go on working steadily day by day, quite quietly, to be prepared for mistakes, which are inevitable, and for failures."

I believed those words then, and I believe them now, though in the intervening years my faith in them has often been tested. After the success of my first novels I was *not* prepared for rejections, for the long years of failure. Again I turned to Tchekov: "The thought that I must, that I ought to, write, never leaves me for an instant." Alas, it *did* leave me, when I had attacks of false guilt because I was spending so much time at the typewriter and in no way pulling my own weight financially. But it never left me for long.

I've written about that decade of failure in *A Circle of Quiet*. I learned a lot of valuable lessons during that time, but there's no doubt that they were bitter. This past winter I wrote in my journal, "If I'd read these words of Rilke's during the long years of rejection they might have helped, because I could have answered the question in the affirmative:

You are looking outward, and that above all you should not do now. Nobody can counsel and help you, nobody. There is only one single way. Go into yourself. Search for the reason that bids you to write; find out whether it is spreading out its roots in the deepest places of your heart, acknowledge to yourself whether you would have to die if it were denied you to write. This above all—ask yourself in the stillest hour of your night: *Must* I write? Delve into yourself for a deep answer. And if this should be affirmative, if you may meet this earnest question with a strong and simple "I must," then build your life according to this necessity; your life even into its most indifferent and slightest hour must be a sign of this urge and testimony to it.

That is from *Letters to a Young Poet,* and surely Rilke speaks to all of us who struggle with a vocation of words.

The writer does want to be published; the painter urgently hopes that someone will see the finished canvas (van Gogh was denied the satisfaction of having his work bought and appreciated during his lifetime; no wonder the pain was more than he could bear); the composer needs his music to be heard. Art is communication, and if there is no communication it is as though the work had been stillborn.

The reader, viewer, listener, usually grossly underestimates his importance. If a reader cannot create a book along with the writer, the book will never come to life. Creative involvement: that's the basic difference between reading a book and watching TV. In watching TV we are passive; sponges; we *do* nothing. In reading we must become creators. Once the child has learned to read alone and can pick up a book without illustrations, he must become a creator, imagining the setting of the story, visualizing the characters, seeing facial expressions, hearing the inflection of voices. The author and the reader "know" each other; they meet on the bridge of words.

So there is no evading the fact that the artist yearns for success, because that means that there has been a communication of the vision: that all the struggle has not been invalid.

Yet with each book I write I am weighted with a deep longing for anonymity, a feeling that books should not be signed, reviews should not be read. But I sign the books; I read the reviews.

Two writers I admire express the two sides of this paradox. They seem to disagree with each other completely, and yet I believe that each is right.

E. M. Forster writes,

> . . . all literature tends towards a condition of anonymity, and that, so far as words are creative, a signature merely distracts from their true significance.
>
> I do not say that literature "ought" not to be signed . . . because literature is alive, and consequently "ought" is the wrong word. It wants not to be signed. That is my point. It is always tugging in that direction . . . saying, in effect, "I,

not the author, really exist."

The poet wrote the poem, no doubt. But he forgot himself while he wrote it, and we forget him while we read. . . . We forget, for ten minutes, his name and our own, and I contend that this temporary forgetfulness, this momentary and mutual anonymity, is sure evidence of good stuff.

Modern education promotes the unmitigated study of literature, and concentrates our attention on the relation between a writer's life—his surface life—and his work. That is the reason it is such a curse.

Literature wants not to be signed.

And yet I know whom I am quoting, for Forster signed his work.

W. H. Auden writes:

Our judgment of an established author is never simply an aesthetic judgment. In addition to any literary merit it may have, a new book by him has a historic interest for us as the act of a person in whom we have long been interested. He is not only a poet or a novelist; he is also a character in our biography.

We cannot seem to escape paradox; I do not think I want to.

Forster refers to "*his* surface life and *his* work"; Auden says, "*He* is not only a poet or a novelist; *he* is also a character in our biography." That *his*

and that *he* refers as much to Jane Austen and George Sand as to Flaubert and Hemingway. It is a generic *his* and *he,* and not exclusively masculine.

I am a female of the species man. Genesis is very explicit that it takes both male and female to make the image of God, and that the generic word *man* includes both.

God created man in his own image, male and female.

That is Scripture, therefore I refuse to be timid about being part of *man*kind. We of the female sex are half of mankind, and it is pusillanimous to resort to he/she, him/her, or even worse, android words. I have a hunch that those who would do so have forgotten their rightful heritage.

I know that I am fortunate in having grown up in a household where no sexist roles were imposed on me. I lived in an atmosphere which assumed equality with all its differences. When mankind was referred to it never occurred to me that I was not part of it or that I was in some way being excluded. My great-great-grandmother, growing up on the St. John's River in times of violence and hardship, had seven homes burned down; nevertheless she spoke casually in seven languages. Her daughter-in-law ran a military hospital, having been brought up at the court of Spain, where she was her ambassador father's hostess; her closest friend was the princess Eugenie, soon to be empress, and the two young women rode and competed with the princess's brothers in all sports; to prove their bravery, each drove a sharp knife into the flesh of the forearm without whimper. Others of my female forebears crossed the country in covered wagons and knew how to handle a gun as well as any man.

Perhaps it is this background which has made me assume casually that of course I am not excluded when anyone refers to a novelist—or anyone else— as *he* or *him*. My closest woman friend is a physician, and so is my daughter-in-law. Not all women have been as fortunate as I have been. When my books were being rejected during the fifties it was not because of my sex, it was because the editors did not like what I was writing. My words were being rejected, not my femaleness.

Because I am a storyteller I live by words. Perhaps music is a purer art form. It may be that when we communicate with life on another planet, it will be through music, not through language or words.

But I am a storyteller, and that involves language, for me the English language, that wonderfully rich, complex, and ofttimes confusing tongue. When language is limited, I am thereby diminished, too.

In time of war language always dwindles, vocabulary is lost; and we live in a century of war. When I took my elder daughter's tenth-grade vocabulary cards up to the school from which she had graduated, less than a decade after she had left, the present tenth-grade students knew almost none of them. It was far easier for my daughter to read Shakespeare in high school than it was for students coming along just a few years after her.

This diminution is worldwide. In Japan, after the Second World War, so many written characters were lost that it is difficult, if not impossible, for the present-day college student to read the works of the great classical masters. In the USSR, even if Solzhenitsyn had been allowed to be read freely, it would not have been easy for the average student to read his novels, for again, after revolution and war, vocabulary fell away. In one of Solzhenitsyn's books his hero spends hours at night reading the great Russian dictionary which came out in the late nineteenth century, and Solzhenitsyn himself draws on this work, and in his writing he is redeeming language, using the words of Tolstoy and Dostoyevsky, using the words of the people of the street, bringing language back to life as he writes.

So it has always been. Dante, writing in exile when dukedoms and principalities were embroiled in wars, was forging language as he wrote his great science-fiction fantasies.

We think because we have words, not the other way around. The more words we have, the better able we are to think conceptually. Yet another reason why *Wrinkle* was so often rejected is that there are many words in it which would never be found on a controlled vocabulary list for the age-group of the ten-to-fourteen-year-old. *Tesseract*, for instance. It's a real word, and one essential for the story.

As a child, when I came across a word I didn't know, I didn't stop reading the story to look it up, I just went on reading. And after I had come across the word in several books, I knew what it meant; it had been added to my vocabulary. This still happens. When I started to read Teilhard de Chardin's *The Phenomenon of Man*, I was determined to understand it. I read intelligently, with a dictionary beside me, stopping to look up the scientific words which were not familiar to me. And I bogged down. So I put aside the dictionary and read as though I were reading a story, and quickly I got drawn into the book, fascinated by his loving theology, and understood it far better, at a deeper level, than if I had stuck with the dictionary.

Is this contradiction? I don't think so. We played with my daughter's vocabulary words during dinner. We kept a dictionary by the table, just for fun. But when we read, we read. We were capable of absorbing far more vocabulary when we read straight on than when we stopped to look up every word. Sometimes I will jot down words to be looked up later. But we learn words in many ways, and much of my vocabulary has been absorbed by my subconscious mind, which then kindly blips it up to my conscious mind when it is needed.

We cannot Name or be Named without language. If our vocabulary dwindles to a few shopworn words, we are setting ourselves up for takeover by a dictator. When language becomes exhausted, our freedom dwindles—we cannot think; we do not recognize danger; injustice strikes us as no more than "the way things are."

Some of the Ayia Napa delegates came from countries ruled by dictators, either from the right or the left. In both cases, teachers are suspect; writers are suspect because people who use words are able to work out complex ideas, to see injustice, and perhaps even to try to do something about it. Simply being able to read the Bible in their own language made some of the delegates suspect.

I might even go to the extreme of declaring that the deliberate diminution of vocabulary by a dictator, or an advertising copy writer, is anti-Christian.

One cannot have been brought up on the *Book of Common Prayer,* as I was, and not have a feeling for language, willy-nilly. In my first boarding school we had mandatory Morning and Evening Prayer, through which we sat, bored, looking for divertissement, ready to snicker if someone broke wind or belched. But the language of Cranmer and Coverdale could not but seep through the interstices. Ready and willing or not, we were enriched.

It is not surprising that there has been considerable discussion about the *New Episcopal Book of Common Prayer,* in church circles, Protestant and Roman Catholic, and by Everyman as well. The language of the *Book of Common Prayer* is part of our literary heritage, as is the language of the King James translation of the Bible. Writers throughout centuries of literature have drawn from the *Prayer Book* as well as the Bible—how many titles come from the Psalms! Novels often contain sentences from Scripture without identification, because it is part of our common heritage; there is no need for footnoting.

There was much in the 1928 *Book of Common Prayer* which needed changing; indeed, revision was first talked about in the year of publication. So it is not that all the critics of the new translations are against change (though some are), but against shabby language, against settling for the mediocre and the flabbily permissive. Where language is weak, theology is weakened.

I do not want to go back to the 1928 *Prayer Book.* We can't "go home again." On the whole, the new *Prayer Book* is a vast improvement over the '28. But I do want us to be aware that not only the '28 *Prayer Book* had flaws. What has been gained in strength of structure has been lost in poverty of language. Some of the translations of Cranmer's Collects (those magnificent, one-sentence petitions) or Coverdale's psalms remind me of what Bowdler did to Shakespeare. Well, Bowdler had his way for a while, but we went back to the richness of Shakespeare.

There are some elegant sentences in the new translation ("I myself will awaken the dawn"), but some verses aren't much better than a French translation of *Hamlet*, in which the famous words Hamlet utters when he first sees the ghost of his father, "Angels and ministers of grace defend us," are rendered, "Tiens, qu'est que c'est que ça?" And surely Shakespeare's words prove his familiarity with Scripture, for they are reminiscent of Saul's encounter with the ghost of Samuel.

Pelican in the wilderness has now become *vulture. Praise him, dragons and all deeps,* has become *sea monsters,* which lacks alliteration, to put it mildly. I have been using the new *Book* for—approximately ten years, I think. It is now thoroughly familiar. In the old language I read, "Be ye sure that the Lord he is God; it is he that hath made us, and not we ourselves." That is a lot more potent theology than "For the Lord himself has made us and we are his." True. But we also need to be reminded in this do-it-yourself age that it is indeed God who has made us and not we ourselves. We are human and humble and of the earth, and we cannot create until we acknowledge our createdness.

In the old language I read, "O God, make clean our hearts within us, and take not thy Holy Spirit from us." In the new version it is, "Create clean hearts within us, O Lord, and comfort us with your Holy Spirit." All very well, but we need to know that if we turn from God, if we are rebellious and stiff-necked we deeply offend the Holy Spirit; we may not take him for granted; he indwells us on his own conditions, not ours. We cannot simply ingest him when we feel like it, like an aspirin.

Although *Holy Ghost* has been rendered as *Holy Spirit* throughout, there seems to be considerable fear of the word *Spirit* and all its implications:

To "The Lord be with you," we used to reply, "And with thy spirit."

Now it goes, "The Lord be with you." "And also with you."

To which the only suitable response is, "Likewise, I'm sure."

We're told that the new *Prayer Book* is meant to be in "the language of the people." But which people? And in language which is left after a century of war, all dwindled and shrivelled? Are we supposed to bring our language down to the lowest common denominator in order to be "meaningful"? And, if we want to make the language contemporary, why not just cut out the *thy* and say, "And with your spirit?" Why are we afraid of the word *spirit?* Does it remind us of baffling and incomprehensible and fearful things like the Annunciation and the Transfiguration and the Passover, those mighty acts of God which we forget how to understand because our childlike creativity has been corrupted and diminished?

Perhaps the old *Prayer Book* dwelt too much on penitence, but there was also excellent psychology in confessing, "We have left undone those things which we ought to have done," *before* "We have done those things which we ought not to have done." In the new confession we confess our sins of commission before our sins of omission. But I have noticed that when someone dies, those who are left are apt to cry out, "Oh, if I had only taken her on that picnic!" or, "If only I'd gone to see him last Wednesday." It is the things I have left undone which haunt me far more than the things which I have done.

In restricting the language in the new translations we have lost that depth and breadth which can give us the kind of *knowing* which is our heritage. This loss has permeated our literature and our prayers, not necessarily in that order. College students of the future will miss many allusions in their surveys of English literature because the language of the great seventeenth-century translators is no longer in their blood stream. I like to read the new translations of Bible and *Prayer Book* for new insights, for shocks of discovery and humour, but I don't want to discard the old, as though it were as transitory as last year's fashions.

Nor do I want to be stuck in the vague android-ism which has resulted from the attempts to avoid the masculine pronoun. We are in a state of intense sexual confusion, both in life and language, but the social manipulation is not working. Language is a living thing; it does not stay the same; it is hard for me to read the language of *Piers Plowman*, for instance, so radical have the changes been. But language is its own creature. It evolves on its own. It follows the language of its great artists, such as Chaucer. It does not do well when suffering from arbitrary control. Our attempts to change the words which have long been part of a society dominated by males have not been successful; instead of making language less sexist they have made it more so.

Indeed we are in a bind. For thousands of years we have lived in a paternalistic society, where women have allowed men to make God over in their own masculine image. But that's anthropomorphism. To think of God in terms of sex at all is a dead end.

To substitute *person* for *man* has ruined what used to be a good theological word, calling up the glory of God's image within us. Now, at best, it's a joke. There's something humiliating and embarrassing about being a chairperson. Or a chair. A group of earnest women have put together a volume of desexed hymns, and one of my old favourites now begins:

"Dear Mother-Father of personkind . . ."

No. It won't do. This is not equality. Perhaps we should drop the word *woman* altogether and use man, recognizing that we need both male and female to be whole. And perhaps if we ever have real equality with all our glorious differences, the language itself will make the appropriate changes. For language, like a story or a painting, is alive. Ultimately it will be the artists who will change the language (as Chaucer did, as Dante did, as Joyce did), not the committees. For an artist is not a consumer, as our commercials urge us to be. An artist is a nourisher and a creator who knows that during the act of creation there is collaboration. We do not create alone.

A friend of mine at a denominational college reported sadly that one of his students came to complain to him about a visiting professor. This professor was having the students read some twentieth century fiction, and the student was upset at both the language of this fiction and the amount of what she considered to be immoral sex.

My friend, knowing the visiting professor to be a person of both intelligence and integrity, urged the student to go and talk with him about these concerns.

"Oh, I couldn't do that," the student said. "He isn't a Christian."

"He" is a Roman Catholic.

If we fall into Satan's trap of assuming that other people are not Christians because they do not belong to our own particular brand of Christianity, no wonder we become incapable of understanding the works of art produced by so-called non-Christians, whether they be atheists, Jews, Buddhists, or anything else outside a frame of reference we have made into a closed rather than an open door.

If I cannot see evidence of incarnation in a painting of a bridge in the rain by Hokusai, a book by Chaim Potok or Isaac Bashevis Singer, music by Bloch or Bernstein, then I will miss its significance in an Annunciation by Franciabigio, the final chorus of the St. Matthew Passion, the words of a sermon by John Donne.

One of the most profoundly moving moments at Ayia Napa came for me when Jesse, a student from Zimbabwe, told me, "I am a good Seventh Day Adventist, but you have shown me God." Jesse will continue to be a good Seventh Day Adventist as he returns to Africa to his family; I will struggle with my own way of belief; neither of us felt the need or desire to change the other's Christian frame of reference. For that moment, at least, all our doors and windows were wide open; we were not carefully shutting out God's purifying light in order to feel safe and secure; we were bathed in the same light that burned and yet did not consume the bush. We walked barefoot on holy ground.

I happen to love spinach, but my husband, Hugh, does not; he prefers beets, which I don't much care for—except the greens. Neither of us thinks less of the other because of this difference in taste. Both spinach and beets are vegetables; both are good for us. We do not have to enjoy precisely the same form of balanced meal.

We also approach God in rather different ways, but it is the same God we are seeking, just as Jesse and I, in our totally different disciplines, worship the same Lord.

Stories, no matter how simple, can be vehicles of truth; can be, in fact, icons. It's no coincidence that Jesus taught almost entirely by telling stories, simple stories dealing with the stuff of life familiar to the Jews of his day. Stories are able to help us to become more whole, to become Named. And Naming is one of the impulses behind all art; to give a name to the cosmos we see despite all the chaos.

God asked Adam to name all the animals, which was asking Adam to help in the creation of their wholeness. When we name each other, we are sharing in the joy and privilege of incarnation, and all great works of art are icons of Naming.

When we look at a painting or hear a symphony or read a book and feel more Named, then, for us, that work is a work of Christian art. But to look at a work of art and then to make a judgment as to whether or not it is art, and whether or not it is Christian, is presumptious. It is something we cannot know in any conclusive way. We can know only if it speaks within our own hearts and leads us to living more deeply with Christ in God.

One of my professors, Dr. Caroline Gordon, a deeply Christian woman, told our class, "We do not judge great art. It judges us." And that very judgment may enable us to change our lives and to renew our commitment to the Lord of Creation.

But how difficult it is for us not to judge; to make what, in the current jargon, is called "a value judgment"! And here we blunder into paradox again. Jesus said, "Judge not, that you be not judged." And yet daily we must make decisions which involve judgments:

We had peanut-butter sandwiches yesterday because they are Tod's favourites. Today it's Sarah's turn, and we'll have bologna with lots of mustard.

I will not let my child take this book of fairy tales out of the library because fairy tales are untrue.

I will share these wonderful fairy tales with my child because they are vehicles of hidden truths.

I will not talk with the Roman Catholic professor lest he make me less Christian than I think I am.

I will not talk to the Jewish scientist in the next apartment or Hitler and the Storm Troopers might send me to a concentration camp.

I will not read this book because it might shake my belief in the answers I am so comfortable with.

Zeal for thine house hath eaten me up.

But Bertrand Russell says, "Zeal is a bad mark for a cause. Nobody has any zeal about arithmetic. It is not the vaccinationists but the antivaccinationists who generate zeal. People are zealous for a cause when they are not quite positive that it is true."

It is hard for us to believe now that there were antivaccinationists, when vaccinations have succeeded in wiping smallpox from the planet. It is hard for us to believe that Dr. Semmelweis was almost torn to pieces when he suggested that physicians should wash their hands before delivering babies in order to help prevent the septicemia or puerperal fever which killed so many women after childbirth. It is hard for us to believe that Bach was considered heretical when he put the thumb under instead of over the fingers on the keyboard. It is hard for us to believe that Shakespeare was considered a trivial playwright because he was too popular. But great negative zeal was expended in all of these cases.

We all tend to make zealous judgments and thereby close ourselves off from revelation. If we feel that we already know something in its totality, then we fail to keep our ears and eyes open to that which may expand or even change that which we so zealously think we know.

My non-Christian friends and acquaintances are zealous in what they "know" about Christianity, which bears little or no relationship to anything I believe.

A friend of mine, Betty Beckwith, in her book, *If I Had the Wings of the Morning*, writes about taking her brain-damaged child to a Jewish doctor. He said, "You people think of us as the people who killed your Christ." Spontaneously she replied, "Oh, no. We think of you as the people who gave him to us."

In the literary world today, Christianity has pretty well replaced sex as the present pet taboo, not only because Christianity is so often distorted by Christians as well as non-Christians, but because it is too wild and free for the timid.

How many of us really want life, life more abundant, life which does not promise any fringe benefits or early retirement plans? Life which does not promise the absence of pain, or love which is not vulnerable and open to hurt? The number of people who attempt to withdraw from life through the abuse of alcohol, tranquilizers, barbiturates is statistically shocking.

How many of us dare to open ourselves to that truth which would make us free? Free to talk to Roman Catholics or charismatics or Jews, as Jesus was free to talk to tax collectors or publicans or Samaritans. Free to feast at the Lord's table with those whose understanding of the Body and Blood may be a little different from ours. Free to listen to angels. Free to run across the lake when we are called.

What is a true icon of God to one person may be blasphemy to another. And it is not possible for us flawed human beings to make absolute zealous judgments as to what is and what is not religious art. I know what is religious art for me. You know what is religious art for you. And they are not necessarily the same. Not everybody feels pulled up to heavenly heights in listening to the pellucid, mathematically precise structure of a Bach fugue. The smarmy picture of Jesus which I find nauseating may be for someone else a true icon.

Another problem about identifying what is and what is not religious art is that religious art transcends its culture and reflects the eternal, and while we are alive we are caught within our culture. All artists reflect the time in which they live, but whether or not their work also has that universality which lives in any generation or culture is nothing we can know for many years. Also, art which is truly iconographic for one period may have little to say to another. My parents, who were in their thirties at the time of the First World War, loved Romantic music, Chopin, Wagner—how they loved Wagner! But Wagner has little to say to me. The reasonable, peaceful world in which my parents grew up, the world which was far too civilized for war, was broken forever by the horror of World War I. My father went to fight in the war to end war, and for the rest of his life he had to live with the knowledge that not only had his war not ended war, it was the beginning of a century of near-total war.

My generation, and my children's, living in this embattled and insane period, finds more nourishment in the structure of Bach and Mozart than in the lush romanticism of Wagner. Wagner is fine if the world around one is stable. But when the world is, indeed, in chaos, then an affirmation of cosmos becomes essential.

Usually, after the death of a well-known artist, there comes a period of eclipse of his work. If the artist reflects only his own culture, then his works will die with that culture. But if his works reflect the eternal and universal, they will revive. It's difficult to believe that for several centuries after Shakespeare's death he was virtually unknown. William Green, his contemporary, was considered a better playwright than the too-popular Will, who pandered to public taste. But was it pandering? Art should communicate with as many people as possible, not just with a group of the esoteric elite. And who remembers Green today?

Bach, too, was eclipsed and remembered as a good church organist rather than a composer, and for a long time that putting of the thumb under the fingers was held against him; no wonder the thumb had been very little used in keyboard music until Bach came along with this "radical" departure from custom.

Bach might have been forgotten forever had not Mendelssohn discovered some monks wrapping parcels in music manuscript—and given the St. Matthew Passion back to the world.

The St. Matthew Passion is an icon of the highest quality for me, an open door into the realm of the numinous. Bach, of course, was a man of deep and profound religious faith, a faith which shines through his most secular music. As a matter of fact, the melody of his moving chorale *O sacred head now wounded* was the melody of a popular street song of the day, but Bach's religious genius was so great that it is now recognized as one of the most superb pieces of religious music ever written.

There is nothing so secular that it cannot be sacred, and that is one of the deepest messages of the Incarnation.

CHAPTER THREE

HEALED, WHOLE AND HOLY

All children are artists, and it is an indictment of our culture that so many of them lose their creativity, their unfettered imaginations, as they grow older. But they start off without self-consciousness as they paint their purple flowers, their anatomically impossible people, their thunderous, sulphurous skies. They don't worry that they may not be as good as Di Chirico or Bracque; they know intuitively that it is folly to make comparisons, and they go ahead and say what they want to say. What looks like a hat to a grownup may, to the child artist, be an elephant inside a boa constrictor.

So what happens? Why do we lose our wonderful, racketty creativity? What corrupts us?

Corrupt: another unpopular word; another important one. Its importance first struck me when I was reading Thomas Traherne, one of my favourite

seventeenth-century poets and mystics. "Certainly
Adam and Eve in Paradise had not more sweete and
curious apprehensions of the world than I when I
was a child," he wrote. Everything was new and
delightful for him. The rosy glow of sunrise had in
it the flaming glory of creation. The stars at night
were a living, heavenly dance. He listened to the
grass growing, smelled the west wind, tasted the
rain, touched the grains of sand on the shore. All
his senses, his mind, his heart, were alive and in
touch with *being*. "So that," Traherne adds sadly,
"without much ado I was corrupted, and made to
learn the dirty devices of this world, which now I
unlearn, and become as it were a little child again,
that I may enter into the kingdom of God."

A lot of my adult life has been spent in trying to
overcome this corruption, in unlearning the dirty
devices of this world, which would dull our imaginations, cut away our creativity. So it is only with
the conscious-unself-consciousness of a child that I
can think about theories of aesthetics, of art, particularly as these touch upon my questions about
life and love and God.

I was still at the age of unself-conscious spontaneity
when I started to write. At the age of five I wrote
a story, which my mother saved for a long time,
about a little "grul," my five-year-old spelling for
girl.

I wrote stories because I was a solitary, only child
in New York City, with no easily available library
where I could get books. So when I had read all

the stories in my bookcase, the only way for me to get more stories to read was to write them.

And I knew, as a child, that it was through story that I was able to make some small sense of the confusions and complications of life. The sound of coughing from my father's gas-burned lungs was a constant reminder of war and its terror. At school I read a book about the Belgian babies impaled on bayonets like small, slaughtered animals. I saw pictures of villages ravaged by the *Bôches*. The thought that there could ever be another war was a source of deep fear. I would implore my parents, "There won't be another war, will there?" My parents never lied to me. They tried to prepare me for this century of war, not to frighten me.

But I was frightened, and I tried to heal my fear with stories, stories which gave me courage, stories which affirmed that ultimately love is stronger than hate. If love is stronger than hate, then war is not all there is. I wrote, and I illustrated my stories. At bedtime my mother told me more stories. And so story helped me to learn to live. Story was in no way an evasion of life, but a way of living life creatively instead of fearfully.

It was a shock when one day in school one of the teachers accused me of "telling a story." She was not complimenting me on my fertile imagination. She was making the deadly accusation that I was telling a lie.

If I learned anything from that teacher, it was that lie and story are incompatible. If it holds no truth, then it cannot truly be story. And so I knew that it was in story that I found flashes of that truth which makes us free.

And yet we are still being taught that fairy tales and myths are to be discarded as soon as we are old enough to understand "reality." I received a disturbed and angry letter from a young mother who told me that a friend of hers, with young children, gave them only instructive books; she wasn't going to allow their minds to be polluted with fairy tales. They were going to be taught the "real" world.

This attitude is a victory for the powers of this world. A friend of mine, a fine storyteller, remarked to me, "Jesus was not a theologian. He was God who told stories."

Yes. God who told stories.

St. Matthew says, "And he spake many things unto them in parables . . . and without a parable spake he not unto them."

When the powers of this world denigrate and deny the value of story, life loses much of its meaning; and for many people in the world today, life *has* lost its meaning, one reason why every other hospital bed is for someone with a mental, not a physical, illness.

Clyde Kilby writes, "Meaninglessness inhibits fullness of life and is therefore equivalent to illness. Meaning makes a great many things endurable—perhaps everything. . . . it is not that 'God' is a myth, but that myth is the revelation of a divine life in man. It is not we who invent myth; rather, it speaks to us as a Word of God."

The well-intentioned mothers who don't want their children polluted by fairy tales would not only deny them their childhood, with its high creativity, but they would have them conform to the secular world, with its dirty devices. The world of fairy tale, fantasy, myth, is inimical to the secular world, and in total opposition to it, for it is interested not in limited laboratory proofs but in truth.

When I was a child, reading Hans Christian Andersen's tales, reading about Joseph and his coat of many colours and his infuriating bragging about his dreams, reading *The Selfish Giant* and *The Book of Jonah*, these diverse stories spoke to me in the same language, and I knew intuitively that they belonged to the same world. For the world of the Bible, both the Old and New Testaments, is the world of story, story which may be able to speak to us as a Word of God.

The artist who is a Christian, like any other Christian, is required to be *in* this world, but not *of* it. We are to be in this world as healers, as listeners, and as servants.

In art we are once again able to do all the things we have forgotten; we are able to walk on water; we speak to the angels who call us; we move, unfettered, among the stars.

We write, we make music, we draw pictures, because we are listening for meaning, feeling for healing. And during the writing of the story or the painting or the composing or singing or playing, we are returned to that open creativity which was ours when we were children. We cannot be mature artists if we have lost the ability to believe which we had as children. An artist at work is in a condition of complete and total faith.

Bach is, for me, the Christian artist *par excellence,* and if I ask myself why, I think it has something to do with his sense of newness. I've been working on his C Minor Toccata and Fugue since college, and I find something new in it every day. And perhaps this is because God was new for Bach every day, was never taken for granted. Too often we do take God for granted. I'm accustomed to being a Christian. I was born of Christian parents who were born of Christian parents who were . . .

That's all right when one is a child, that comfortable familiarity with being Christian, because to the child, as to Thomas Traherne when he was small, everything is wonderful and new, even familiarity. The edge has not been taken off the glory of God's creation. But later on there comes a time when this very familiarity can become one of those corrupting devices. We learn this early, in our attachment to certain bedtime routines of bath and story and prayer and teddy bear and glass of water and goodnight kiss—and the routine must never be varied because this is security in what the child learns early is an insecure world.

This past winter, while our three grandchildren were with us because their parents were in the Holy Land, I knew the joy again of a bedtime routine with a two-and-a-half-year-old. Edward and I sang "Molly Malone" and "Speed Bonny Boat" at the piano. Then came bath and bed and more songs, and finally the great moment of the bedtime routine came when he looked at his great-grandmother's charm bracelet, and particularly a small, silver wicker basket, which we opened with extreme care, for within it was the baby Moses. The basket was the basket of bullrushes in which Moses' mother put him in the river, that he might be found by Pharoah's daughter. Edward would hold this tiny metal baby, less than a centimeter long, and look at it wonderingly, and every night he would say, "He will grow up to be a great prince."

The child himself will know when it is time to let this safe routine go, when holding the soft corner of the favourite blanket is no longer needed for sleep, when the most dearly loved stuffed animal can stay in the toy chest. It is a mistake for the parent to try too abruptly to break the pattern. Most children will let it go when the right time comes. But there are other and less creative familiarities which remain with us and dull our perceptions. When we lose waking up in the morning as though each day was going to be full of adventure, joys, and dangers, and wake up instead to the alarm clock (as most of us must, and how lovely those rare nights when we look at the clock and don't have to set the alarm), and the daily grind, and mutter about TGIF, we lose the newborn quality of belief which is so lovely in the child. It may be less lovely in the artist; it can occasionally be infuriating; but without it there is no impulse to rush to the canvas to set down that extraordinary smile; to catch the melody in the intricacies of a fugue) to reach out to life and then see Hamlet pull back, and wonder why.

Along with reawakening the sense of newness, Bach's music points me to wholeness, a wholeness of body, mind, and spirit, which we seldom glimpse, but which we are intended to know. It is no coincidence that the root word of *whole, health, heal, holy,* is *hale* (as in *hale and hearty)*. If we are healed, we become whole; we are hale and hearty; we are holy.

The marvellous thing is that this holiness is nothing we can earn. We don't become holy by acquiring merit badges and Brownie points. It has nothing to do with virtue or job descriptions or morality. It is nothing we can *do* in this do-it-yourself world. It is gift, sheer gift, waiting there to be recognized and received. We do not have to be qualified to be holy. We do not have to be qualified to be whole, or healed.

The fact that I am not qualified was rammed into me early, and though this hurt, it was salutary. As a small child I was lonely not only because I was an only child in a big city but because I was slightly lame, extremely introverted, and anything but popular at school. There was no question in my mind that I was anything but whole, that I did not measure up to the standards of my peers or teachers. And so, intuitively, I turned to writing as a way of groping towards wholeness. I wrote vast quantities of short stories and poetry; I painted and played the piano. I lived far too much in an interior world, but I did learn that I didn't have to be qualified according to the world's standards in order to write my stories. It was far more likely my total *lack* of qualifications that turned me to story to search for meaning and truth, to ask those eternal questions: Why? What is it all about? Does my life have any meaning? Does anybody care?

To try to find the answers to these questions, I not only wrote but also read omnivorously, anything I could get my hands on—fairy tales, the brothers Grimm, Hans Christian Andersen, Oscar Wilde, the story of Tobias and the angel, Gideon and the angel. Very early in my life the Bible taught me to care about angels. I also read about dreams in the Bible, and so I took dreams seriously. I read and reread and reread *Emily of New Moon,* by L. M. Montgomery, author of the more famous stories about *Anne of Green Gables.* I liked the Anne stories, but especially I loved Emily, because she, too, wanted to be a writer, a real writer; she, too, walked to the beat of a different drummer; she had a touch of second sight, that gift which allows us to peek for a moment at the world beyond ordinary space and time.

My lonely solitude kept me far more in touch with this world of the imagination than I would have been had I been off with the other children playing hopscotch or skipping rope. It was this world which gave me assurance of meaning and reality despite the daily world in which I was a misfit, and in which I knew many fears as I overheard my parents talking about the nations once again lining up for war.

If I found this world in *Emily of New Moon,* in books of Chinese fairy tales, as well as in Andrew Lang's collections, I also found it in the Bible stories. I was fortunate (in the strange way in which tragedy brings with it blessings as well as griefs) because my father's deteriorating lungs dictated an unusual schedule; he worked best in the afternoon and evening, and slept late into the morning.

Therefore there was no one to take me to Sunday school. I have talked with such a surprising number of people who have had to spend most of their lives unlearning what some well-meaning person taught them in Sunday school, that I'm glad I escaped! All the old heresies of the first few centuries—Donatism, Manicheism, Docetism, to name but three—are still around, and Satan doesn't hesitate to use them wherever possible.

In the world of literature, Christianity is no longer respectable. When I am referred to in an article or a review as a "practicing Christian" it is seldom meant as a compliment, at least not in the secular press. It is perfectly all right, according to literary critics, to be Jewish or Buddhist or Sufi or a pre-Christian druid. It is not all right to be a Christian. And if we ask why, the answer is a sad one: Christians have given Christianity a bad name. They have let their lights flicker and grow dim. They have confused piosity with piety, smugness with joy. During the difficult period in which I was struggling through my "cloud of unknowing" to return to the church and to Christ, the largest thing which deterred me was that I saw so little clear light coming from those Christians who sought to bring me back to the fold.

But I'm back, and grateful to be back, because, through God's loving grace, I did meet enough people who showed me that light of love which the darkness cannot extinguish. One of the things I learned on the road back is that I do not have to be right. I have to try to do what is right, but when it turns out, as happens with all of us, to be wrong, then I am free to accept that it was wrong, to say,

"I'm sorry," and to try, if possible, to make reparation. But I have to accept the fact that I am often
unwise; that I am not always loving; that I make
mistakes; that I am, in fact, human. And as Christians we are meant to be not less human than other
people but more human, just as Jesus of Nazareth
was more human.

One time I was talking to Canon Tallis, who is
my spiritual director as well as my friend, and I was
deeply grieved about something, and I kept telling
him how woefully I had failed someone I loved,
failed totally, otherwise that person couldn't have
done the wrong that was so destructive. Finally he
looked at me and said calmly, "Who are you to think
you are better than our Lord? After all, he was sin-
gularly unsuccessful with a great many people."

That remark, made to me many years ago, has
stood me in good stead, time and again. I have to
try, but I do not have to succeed. Following Christ
has nothing to do with success as the world sees
success. It has to do with love.

So does the Bible. God's love for his people. All of
us. As the psalmist sings, "God loves *every* man. . . .
He calls *all* the stars by name."

I'm particularly grateful that I was allowed to
read my Bible as I read my other books, to read it
as *story,* that story which is a revelation of truth.
People are sometimes kept from reading the Bible
itself by what they are taught about it, and I'm
grateful that I was able to read the Book with the
same wonder and joy with which I read *The Ice*

Princess or *The Tempest* or about E. Nesbitt's Psammead, that disagreeable and enchanting creature who would have been no surprise to Abraham or Sarah. In Isaiah I read about those dragons who honour him because he gives "waters in the wilderness, and rivers in the desert, to give drink to his people." So it was no surprise to me to read about a mediaeval dragon who was a great pet in the palace; he helped heat water, and on cold winter nights he got into every bed in the palace, by turn, breathing out just enough warmth to take off the chill and make the sheets toasty to get into.

I had an aunt who worried that I lived in an unreal world. But what is real? In the Bible we are constantly being given glimpses of a reality quite different from that taught in school, even in Sunday school. And these glimpses are not given to the qualified; there's the marvel. It may be that the qualified feel no need of them.

We are all asked to do more than we can do. Every hero and heroine of the Bible does more than he would have thought it possible to do, from Gideon to Esther to Mary. Jacob, one of my favorite characters, certainly wasn't qualified. He was a liar and a cheat, and yet he was given the extraordinary vision of angels and archangels ascending and descending a ladder which reached from earth to heaven.

In the first chapter of John's Gospel, Nathanael was given a glimpse of what Jacob saw, or a promise of it, and he wasn't qualified, either. He was narrow minded and unimaginative, and when Philip told him that Jesus of Nazareth was the one they sought, his rather cynical response was, "Can anything good come out of Nazareth?" And yet it was to Nathanael that Jesus promised the vision of angels and archangels ascending and descending upon the Son of Man.

In the novels and stories which have always meant the most to me, and to which, as both child and adult, I return and return, I find the same thing: the unqualified younger son finishes the quest where the qualified elder brothers fail because they think they can do it themselves. In *Twelfth Night*, Viola, a young, unqualified girl, ends up solving all the tangled problems and marrying the duke. The Macbeths bring disaster on themselves and others because they take things into their own hands; they think they have a *right* to do what they need to do in order for Macbeth to get the crown; they listen to the witches, and they fall for the three temptations of power—temptations which have been the same since Satan offered them to Jesus in the wilderness. King Lear moves into tragedy when he assumes that he has a right to be loved by his daughters and when he tries to compare their love quantitatively.

Moses wasn't qualified (as I run over my favourite characters in both Old and New Testaments, I can't find one who was in any worldly way qualified to do the job which was nevertheless accomplished); Moses was past middle age when God called him to lead his children out of Egypt, and he spoke with a stutter. He was reluctant and unwilling, and he couldn't control his temper. But he saw the bush that burned and was not consumed. He spoke with God in the cloud on Mount Sinai, and afterwards his face glowed with such brilliant light that the people could not bear to look at him.

In a very real sense not one of us is qualified, but it seems that God continually chooses the most unqualified to do his work, to bear his glory. If we are qualified, we tend to think that we have done the job ourselves. If we are forced to accept our evident lack of qualification, then there's no danger that we will confuse God's work with our own, or God's glory with our own.

It is interesting to note how many artists have had physical problems to overcome, deformities, lameness, terrible loneliness. Could Beethoven have written that glorious paean of praise in the Ninth Symphony if he had not had to endure the dark closing in of deafness? As I look through his work chronologically, there's no denying that it deepens and strengthens along with the deafness. Could Milton have seen all that he sees in *Paradise Lost* if he had not been blind? It is chastening to realize that those who have no physical flaw, who move through life in step with their peers, who are bright and beautiful, seldom become artists. The unending paradox is that we do learn through pain.

My mother's long life had more than its fair share of pain and tragedy. One time, after something difficult had happened, one of her childhood friends came to give comfort and help. Instead of which, she burst into tears and sobbed out, "I envy you! I envy you! You've had a terrible life, but you've *lived!*"

I look back at my mother's life and I see suffering deepening and strengthening it. In some people I have also seen it destroy. Pain is not always creative; received wrongly, it can lead to alcoholism and madness and suicide. Nevertheless, without it we do not grow.

Demetrios Capetenakis says, "One must really be brave to choose love or writing as one's guides, because they may lead one to the space in which the meaning of our life is hidden—and who can say that this space may not be the land of death."

Even to the Christian this land of death is dark and frightening. No matter how deep the faith, we each have to walk the lonesome valley; we each have to walk it all alone. The world tempts us to draw back, tempts us to believe we will not have to take this test. We are tempted to try to avoid not only our own suffering but also that of our fellow human beings, the suffering of the world, which is part of our own suffering. But if we draw back from it (and we are free to do so), Kafka reminds us that "it may be that this very holding back is the one evil you could have avoided."

The artist cannot hold back; it is impossible, because writing, or any other discipline of art, involves participation in suffering, in the ills and the occasional stabbing joys that come from being part of the human drama.

We are hurt; we are lonely; and we turn to music or words, and as compensation beyond all price we are given glimpses of the world on the other side of time and space. We all have glimpses of glory as children, and as we grow up we forget them or are taught to think we made them up; they couldn't possibly have been real because to most of us who are grown up, reality is like radium and can be borne only in very small quantities.

But we are meant to be real and to see and recognize the real. We are all more than we know, and that wondrous reality, that wholeness, holiness, is there for all of us, not the qualified only.

I am glad that in the communion of my church we are baptized as infants, because this emphasizes that the gift of death to this world and birth into the kingdom of God is, in fact, gift—it is nothing we have earned, or even, as infants, chosen. It is God's freely bestowed love.

Juan Carlos Ortiz, a priest in South America, uses this baptismal formula: "I kill you in the name of the Father and of the Son and of the Holy Spirit, and I make you born into the kingdom of God to serve and please him."

It is baptism itself that I am talking about, not "immersion" or "splashing." My husband, being properly submerged in the First Baptist Church when he was ten experienced the same undeserved glory that I did, who was baptized before the age of reason. It is the gift that matters. It is death, and life.

It is as radical as that, and it is gift. Through no virtue of our own we are made dead to the old and alive in the new.

And for each one of us there is a special gift, the way in which we may best serve and please the Lord, whose love is so overflowing. And gifts should never be thought of quantitatively. One of the holiest women I have ever known did little with her life in terms of worldly success; her gift was that of bringing laughter with her wherever she went, no matter how dark or grievous the occasion. Wherever she was, holy laughter was present to heal and redeem.

In the Koran it is written, "He deserves Paradise who makes his companions laugh."

CHAPTER FOUR

A COAL IN THE HAND

I am grateful that I started writing at a very early age, before I realized what a daring thing it is to do, to set down words on paper, to attempt to tell a story, create characters. We have to be braver than we think we can be, because God is constantly calling us to be more than we are, to see through plastic sham to living, breathing reality, and to break down our defenses of self-protection in order to be free to receive and give love.

With God, even a rich man can enter the narrow gate to heaven. Earthbound as we are, even we can walk on water.

Paul certainly wasn't qualified to talk about love, Paul who had persecuted so many Christians as ruthlessly as possible; and yet his poem on love in I Corinthians has shattering power. It is not a vague, genial sense of well-being that it offers us but a particular, painful, birth-giving love. How to translate that one word which is the key word? *Charity* long ago lost its original meaning and has come to mean a cold, dutiful giving. And *love* is now almost entirely limited to the narrower forms of sex. Canon Tallis suggests that perhaps for our day the best translation of *love* is the name of Jesus, and that will tell us everything about love we need to know.

It is a listening, unself-conscious love, and many artists who are incapable of this in their daily living are able to find it as they listen to their work, that work which binds our wounds and heals us and helps us toward wholeness.

When I was a child my parents loved me not because I was good but because I was Madeleine, their child. I loved them, and I wanted to please them, but their love of me did not have to be earned.

Neither does the love of God. We are loved because we are his children, because we *are*. The more we feel that we ought to be loved because it is our due or because we deserve it, the less we will truly feel the need of God's love; the less implicit will be our trust; the less will we cry out, *Abba!*

Dostoyevsky writes, in *Crime and Punishment,*

Then Christ will say to us, "Come you as well, Come drunkards, come weaklings, come forth ye children of shame. . . ." And he will say to us,

"Ye are swine, made in the Image of the Beast and with his mark, but come ye also." And the wise men and those of understanding will say: "O Lord, why do you receive these men?" And he will say, "This is why I receive them, O ye of understanding, that not one of them believed himself to be worthy of this." And he will hold out his hands to us and we shall fall down before him . . . and we shall weep . . . and we shall understand all things! Then we shall understand all things! . . . Lord, thy kingdom come.

The root word of *humility* is *humus*, earth; to be *human*, too, comes from the same word; and the parables of Jesus which show the kind of humility he is seeking in us are often earthy, such as the parable of the workers in the vineyard, the parable of the seed and the sower, and the parable of the prodigal son. We all have within us that same lack of humility as the workers who worked in the heat of the day and resented those who got equal pay for shorter hours of work, and we all understand the lack of humility in the elder son who was offended by his father's humble forgiveness.

King Lear's humbleness at the end of his play is all the more moving because it has been born of the pain caused by his arrogance.

And another lovely paradox: we can be humble only when we know that we are God's children, of infinite value, and eternally loved.

The disciples, like the rest of us, did not deserve

God's love, nor their Master's. How must Jesus have felt when he was forced to realize that his disciples, whom he had called to be with him all the way, would not stand with him at the end? Without exception they fled the garden, even John and James and Peter, who had been with him the most. And of the men, only John was at the foot of the cross. The women were there, perhaps because throughout the ages women have been allowed to remain more in touch with the intuitive self than have men, who traditionally have been trained to limit themselves to the rational self. Men are to be strong; able and ready to fight, never to cry; to solve all problems with the rational intellect. While women, involved as they are in the nurture and upbringing of children far more than men, have thereby been helped to retain the child and the dreamer in themselves.

And yet, despite the fear and unfaithfulness of his followers, Jesus' love never faltered, for it was not dependent on the merit and virtue and the qualifications of those he loved.

Wounds. By his wounds we are healed. But they are our wounds, too, and until we have been healed we do not know what wholeness is. The discipline of creation, be it to paint, compose, write, is an effort toward wholeness.

The great male artists have somehow or other retained this wholeness, this being in touch with both intellect and intuition, a wholeness which always has to be bought at a price in this world. How many artists, in the eyes of the world, have been less than whole? Toulouse-Lautrec had the body of a man and the legs of a child. Byron had a club foot. Demosthenes was a terrible stutterer. Traditionally, Homer was blind. The great artists have gained their wholeness through their wounds, their epilepsies, tuberculoses, periods of madness.

My son-in-law, Alan Jones, told me a story of a Hassidic rabbi renowned for his piety. He was unexpectedly confronted one day by one of his devoted youthful disciples. In a burst of feeling, the young disciple exclaimed, "My master, I love you!" The ancient teacher looked up from his books and asked his fervent disciple, "Do you know what hurts me, my son?"

The young man was puzzled. Composing himself, he stuttered, "I don't understand your question, Rabbi. I am trying to tell you how much you mean to me, and you confuse me with irrelevant questions."

"My question is neither confusing nor irrelevant," rejoined the rabbi. "For if you do not know what hurts me, how can you truly love me?"

No matter how much we are hurt, God knows about it, cares about it, and so, through his love, we are sometimes enabled to let go our hurts.

But it is not only our hurts which we are required to give over but our wholenesses, too. It must all be his.

To trust, to be truly whole, is also to let go whatever we may consider our qualifications. There's a paradox here, and a trap for the lazy. I do not need to be "qualified" to play a Bach fugue on the piano (and playing a Bach fugue is for me an exercise in wholeness). But I cannot play that Bach fugue at all if I do not play the piano daily, if I do not practice my finger exercises. There are equivalents of finger exercises in the writing of books, the painting of portraits, the composing of a song. We do not need to be qualified; the gift is free; and yet we have to pay for it.

Isaiah knew himself to be mortal and flawed, but he had the child's courage to say to the Lord, "Here I am. Send me." And he understood the freedom which the Spirit can give us from ordinary restrictions when he wrote, "When you pass through deep waters I am with you; when you pass through rivers, they will not sweep you away; walk through fire and you will not be scorched, through flames and they will not burn you." He may not have had this understanding before he wrote those words, for such understanding is a gift which comes when we let go and listen. I think I looked up this passage because I dreamed that a friend reached into the fireplace and drew out a living coal and held it in his hand, looking at its radiance, and I wondered at him because he was not burned.

It may be that we have lost our ability to hold a blazing coal, to move unfettered through time, to walk on water, because we have been taught that such things have to be earned; we should deserve them; we must be qualified. We are suspicious of grace. We are afraid of the very lavishness of the gift.

But a child rejoices in presents!

Finley Eversole, in *The Politics of Creativity*, writes,

> In our society, at the age of five, 90 percent of the population measures "high creativity." By the age of seven, the figure has dropped to 10 percent. And the percentage of adults with high creativity is only two percent! Our creativity is destroyed not through the use of outside force, but through criticism, innuendo,

by the dirty devices of this world. So we are diminished, and we forget that we are more than we know. The child is aware of unlimited potential, and this munificence is one of the joys of creativity.

Those of us who struggle in our own ways, small or great, trickles or rivers, to create, are constantly having to unlearn what the world would teach us; it is not easy to keep a child's high creativity in these late years of the twentieth century.

It would be only too easy to blame all the dirty devices on the secular world. Some of them, alas, come from the churches, in the form of well-meaning distortions which once sprang from something creative, but which have been changed until they have become destructive.

Truth, for instance: we all want truth, that truth which Jesus promised would make us free. But where do we find it? How could it have happened that even in the church *story* has been lost as a vehicle of truth? Early in our corruption we are taught that fiction is not true. Too many people apologize when they are caught enjoying a book of fiction; they are afraid that it will be considered a waste of time and that they ought to be reading a biography or a book of information on how to pot plants. Is *Jane Eyre* not true? Did Conrad, turning to the writing of fiction in his sixties, not search there for truth? Was Melville, writing about the sea and the great conflict between a man and a whale, not delving for a deeper truth than we can find in any number of how-to books?

And Shakespeare and all the other dramatists before and after him! Are they not revealers of truth? Why then, in some evangelical colleges where I have lectured, are there "Speech Departments," and the students produce and act in plays, but the department cannot be called "theatre," because theatre is wicked and not true?

I have been married to an actor for thirty-four years, and I know him to be a man of total integrity who could not possibly live a life of untruth. I have witnessed his widening knowledge of truth as he has grappled with the characters he has depicted on the stage.

At two colleges during the past year, colleges widely separated geographically, earnest young women have asked me, "How does your husband reconcile being on television with being a Christian?"

My reply is an analogy, a story. I tell them of one time when our children were young and the play my husband was in was closing, and he would shortly be out of work.

He came home from the theatre one night with the script of a new play in which he had been offered a juicy role. He gave it to me to read, and when I had finished, I simply handed it back to him. He nodded. "I wouldn't want the kids to see me in this. I'm not going to take it."

We needed money for rent and food and clothes for our growing children. Hugh needed a job. But the criterion he used was: Would I want the kids to see me in this?

If he didn't care about truth and integrity, what the kids saw him in wouldn't matter.

Perhaps this is an insight into Christian art.

If we try to follow in Jesus' way, what the children see us in *does* matter. Jesus told his friends and disciples over and over again that not only were they to let the little children come to him but that they were to be like little children themselves. When we are like little children, with the openness the child has up until the age for school, then we retain our ability to be creators, our willingness to be open, to believe.

I need not belabour the point that to retain our childlike openness does not mean to be childish. Only the most mature of us are able to be childlike. And to be able to be childlike involves memory; we must never forget any part of ourselves. As of this writing I am sixty-one years old in chronology. But I am not an isolated, chronological numerical statistic. I am sixty-one, and I am also four, and twelve, and fifteen, and twenty-three, and thirty-one, and forty-five, and . . . and . . . and . . .

If we lose any part of ourselves, we are thereby diminished. If I cannot be thirteen and sixty-one simultaneously, part of me has been taken away.

Some of my friends and I have remarked that it would be marvellous if we could go back to college *now*; if we could go back to college and be eighteen again but keep everything we have learned in the intervening years, how much more we would get out of it! The marvellous thing is that in the writing of fiction we can, indeed, be eighteen again, and retain all that has happened to us in our slow growing up. For growing up never ends; we never get there. I am still in the process of growing up, but I will make no progress if I lose any of myself on the way.

We will not have the courage or the ability to unlearn the dirty devices of which Traherne warns us, or to keep our child's creativity, unless we are willing to be truly "grownup." Creativity opens us to revelation, and when our high creativity is lowered to 2 percent, so is our capacity to see angels, to walk on water, to talk with unicorns. In the act of creativity, the artist lets go the self-control which he normally clings to and is open to riding the wind. Something almost always happens to startle us during the act of creating, but not unless we let go our adult intellectual control and become as open as little children. This means not to set aside or discard the intellect but to understand that it is not to become a dictator, for when it does we are closed off from revelation.

Scientists sometimes understand this better than theologians. Dr. Friedrich Dessauer, an atomic physicist, writes,

Man is a creature who depends entirely on revelation. In all his intellectual endeavor, he should always listen, always be intent to hear and see. He should not strive to superimpose the structures of his own mind, his systems of thought upon reality. . . . At the beginning of all spiritual endeavor stands humility, and he who loses it can achieve no other heights than the heights of disillusionment.

Creative scientists and saints expect revelation and do not fear it. Neither do children. But as we grow up and we are hurt, we learn not to trust, and that lack of trust is a wound as grievous as whatever caused it.

It strikes me that perhaps I am elevating scientists and down-grading theologians, and that is not true, nor fair. For the few scientists who live by revelation there are many more who are no more than technicians, who are terrified of the wide world outside the laboratory, and who trust nothing they cannot prove. Amazing things may happen in their test tubes and retorts, but only the rare few see the implications beyond the immediate experiment. They cannot trust further than their own senses, and this lack of trust is often caught by the rest of us.

I was told of a man who had a small son he loved dearly, and so he wanted to protect him against all the things in life which frighten and hurt. He was emphatic in telling the little boy that *nobody* can be trusted. One evening when the father came home, his son came running down the stairs to greet him, and the father stopped him at the landing. "Son," he said, "Daddy has taught you that people are not to be trusted, hasn't he?" "Yes, Daddy." "You can't trust anybody, can you?" "No, Daddy." "But you can trust Daddy, can't you?" "Oh, yes, Daddy." The father then held out his arms and said, "Jump," and the little boy jumped with absolute trust that his father's arms were waiting for him. But the father stepped aside and let the little boy fall crashing to the floor. "You see," he said to his son, "you must trust *no*body."

I trusted my parents, thank God, and I think that my children trust me. We all fail each other; none of us is totally trustworthy; but the more we are trusted, the more we become worthy of trust.

There is much that the artist must trust. He must trust himself. He must trust his work. He must open himself to revelation, and that is an act of trust. The artist must never lose the trust of the child for the parent, not that of the father who knew only the "heights of disillusionment," but the trustworthiness of most of us flawed and fallen parents who nevertheless try to do the best we can for our children.

Jesus told us to call the Lord and Creator of us all *Abba*. Not only Father or Sir or Lord, but Abba—Daddy—the small child's name for Father. Not Dad, the way Daddy becomes Dad when the children reach adolescence, but *Daddy*, the name of trust.

But how can we trust an Abba who has let the world come to all the grief of the past centuries? Who has given us the terrible gift of free will with which we seem to be determined to destroy ourselves?

We trust the one we call Abba as a child does, knowing that what seems unreasonable now will be seen to have reason later. We trust as Lady Julian of Norwich trusted, knowing that despite all the pain and horror of the world, ultimately Gods loving purpose will be fulfilled and "all shall be well and all shall be well and all manner of thing shall be well."

And this *all wellness* underlies true art (Christian art) in all disciplines, an all-wellness that does not come to us because we are clever or virtuous but which is a gift of Grace.

CHAPTER FIVE

PROBABLE IMPOSSIBLES

From Aristotle I learned that a story must have a beginning, a middle, and an end. That, as the Red King advised Alice, it should begin at the beginning, go on to the end, and then stop. That when we are at a play or looking at a painting or a statue or reading a story, the imaginary work must have such an effect on us that it enlarges our own sense of reality.

Let me return to Aristotle's "that which is probable and impossible is better than that which is possible and improbable." I've been chewing on that one since college, and it's all tied in with Coleridge's "willing suspension of disbelief." If the artist can make it probable, we *can* accept the impossible—impossible in man's terms, that is. Aristotle, not knowing the New Testament, could not add, "With man it is impossible; with God nothing is impossible."

The artist at work is less bound by time and space than in ordinary life. But we should be less restricted in ordinary life than we are. We are not supposed to be limited and trapped. As a child it did not seem strange to me that Jesus was able to talk face to face with Moses and Elijah, the centuries between them making no difference.

We are not meant to be as separated as we have become from those who have gone before us and those who will come after. I learned to know and understand my father far more after his death than during his life. Here we are on the border of the tremendous Christian mystery: time is no longer a barrier.

As I read and reread the Gospels, the startling event of the Transfiguration is one of the highlights. You'd think that in the church year we would celebrate it with as much excitement and joy as we do Christmas and Easter. We give it lip service when we talk about "mountaintop experiences," but mostly we ignore it, and my guess is that this is because we are afraid.

A summer or so ago, some Congregational ministers decided chat they would like to go to a church service on this feast day, and checked out the three nearest Episcopal churches. Not one of them was having a celebration. So my son-in-law, Alan, who was on vacation, held a Communion service in the tiny chapel of their home, for the Congregational ministers and some family and friends.

We are afraid of the Transfiguration for much the same reason that people are afraid that theatre is a "lie," that a story isn't "true," that art is somehow immoral, carnal, and not spiritual.

The artist must be open to the wider truths, the shadow side, the strange worlds beyond time. And because God has given his creatures the difficult gift of free will, the artist has more temptations to abuse the gift than—say—the banker or the accountant. Some artists abuse the gift in their private lives while remaining true to it in their work. Some abuse it in their work, and the proliferation of pornographic books and movies is a sad example. The more freedom we are given, the more possibilities we have of abusing this freedom.

We are afraid, and we back off, and some ministers looking for a church service on the Feast of the Transfiguration can't find one.

The Christian holiday which is easiest for us is Christmas because it touches on what is familiar; and the story of the young man and woman who were turned away from the inn and had a baby in a stable, surrounded by gentle animals, is one we have always known. I doubt if many two- or three-year-olds are told at their mother's knee about the Transfiguration or the Annunciation. And so, because the story of Christmas is part of our folklore (we might almost say), we pay more attention to its recognizableness than to the fact that the tiny baby in the manger contained the power which created the galaxies and set the stars in their courses.

We are not taught much about the wilder aspects of Christianity. But these are what artists have wrestled with throughout the years. The Annunciation has been a favourite subject of painter and poets because gestation and birth-giving are basic to any form of creation. All of us who have given birth to a baby, to a story, know that it is ultimately mystery, closely knit to God's own creative activities, which did not stop at the beginning of the universe. God is constantly creating, in us, through us, with us, and to cocreate with God is our human calling. It is the calling for all of us, his creatures, but it is perhaps more conscious with the artist—or should I say the Christian artist?

In literal terms the Annunciation can only confound us. But the whole story of Jesus is confounding to the literal-minded. It might be a good idea if, like the White Queen, we practiced believing six impossible things every morning before breakfast, for we *are* called on to believe what to many people is impossible. Instead of rejoicing in this glorious "impossible" which gives meaning and dignity to our lives, we try to domesticate God, to make his mighty actions comprehensible to our finite minds. It is not that the power to understand is not available to us; it is; he has promised it. But it is a power far greater than the power stations for our greatest cities, and we find it easier not to get too close to it because we know that this power can kill as well as illuminate. Those who try to use it for their own advantage come to disaster, like Simon Magus in the Acts of the Apostles. But then, Simon Magus thought that he was qualified, that power was his due. And this has been the downfall of dictators throughout history, and this century seems to have had an inordinate number of them.

In so-called primitive societies there are two words for power, *mana* and *taboo:* the power which creates and the power which destroys; the power which is benign and the power which is malign. Odd that we have retained in our vocabulary the word for dangerous power, taboo, and have lost mana. Power always has both of these aspects, as the storyteller knows. The sex drive can make love and babies, and it can lead to divorce and murder. The power lines which give us our electricity are mana when we touch a switch in the dark and the room is lit. They are taboo when a fireman on an aluminum ladder slips and his ladder touches a power line and he is electrocuted. It is this double aspect of power which the artist must be brave enough to explore. Sound can ennoble and inspire, as in the case of a Beethoven symphony. A director friend of mine used subliminal sound during the production of a murder play, and on the opening night so many people fainted that he had to cut off the sound which had such a terrifying effect even though it was not consciously heard. A painting of a nude body can glorify the wonder of incarnation or it can titillate and degrade.

This extraordinary power, when it is in the hands of a great genius, is linked with the power which brought the galaxies into being and orchestrated the music of the spheres.

This power, which is impossible for the finite being to grasp in any conclusive fashion, touches on the probable impossible essence of that which is really real. Perhaps for the Christian the Incarnation is the best example of that magnificent "probable impossible." It has been called the "scandal of the particular," for to many people it is scandalous that the Lord of the universe should condescend to come to his people as an ordinary man, with every human restriction. Why would ultimate power choose to limit itself in such a humiliating fashion? Is this really what love is about? The answer to this question has challenged artists throughout the centuries. How can this probable impossible be real?

And what is real? Does the work of art have a reality beyond that of the artist's vision, beyond whatever has been set down on canvas, paper, musical notations? If the artist is the servant of the work, if each work of art, great or small, is the result of an annunciation, then it does.

Hamlet *is*. When the play has been read, when the curtain goes down on the performance, Hamlet still is. He is, in all his ambivalence, as real as Byron or as the man who cried out, "Lord, I believe, help thou my unbelief," or as Ivan Karamazov. The flight of stairs up which George MacDonald's princess had to climb would be there whether or not MacDonald had ever written *The Princess and the Goblin*. The storm still rages around King Lear. The joy of Bach's gigue at the end of the Fifth French Suite does not depend on a piano for its being.

But the reality of the outcome of all annunciations is a reality which is scoffed at by most of the world. It is one of the greater triumphs of Lucifer that he has managed to make Christians

(Christians!) believe that a story is a lie, that a myth should be outgrown with puberty, that to act in a play is inconsistent with true religion.

One of my favourite paintings among El Greco's is a large canvas of St. Francis of Assisi and St. Andrew, which I saw in the Prado, and before which I stood in awed joy, for St. Andrew and St. Francis are companionably talking together, side by side, with the cross between them mediating the distance of eleven hundred years.

And as I set down the word *mediate*, I realized that it is part of the word *immediate*, that place of *now*, where past and future come together.

Those of us who fly a lot know the randomness of time. Two nights in Athens were necessary for me en route to Cyprus because my spirit is able to adjust to the radical time difference more easily than my intestines. Our bodies do not relish having their circadian rhythms disturbed, and that's partly because, over the centuries, we've forgotten how to move about in time, and that particular ability has atrophied.

I'm not sure jet travel is the way we're meant to adapt once again. Technology, for which I am grateful, has too often turned into technocracy, which can become a monster. I'm often asked by people who have read *The Arm of the Starfish* if I believe that experiments like Dr. O'Keefe's on human regeneration will ever become possible. And I can reply that not only do I believe so but that doctors in England have discovered that if a child accidentally loses a finger, the thing to do is not to close the wound or to stitch it up but to keep it clean and open and unbandaged, and *the finger will grow again*. The younger the child, the more rapid will be the regeneration. We are beginning to recognize that medicine has not always done the right thing in turning to the knife or the needle; the human body is far more regenerative than we have realized.

So my feelings about our massive airplanes are part of my feelings about technology-turned-technocracy in general. Surely our machines were not meant to deal out death. More people have been killed in automobile accidents than in all our wars put together: a terrifying statistic.

So I sit in the airport waiting to board my plane, and my storyteller's mind gets to work, and I envision a planet with a civilization more enlightened than ours, where children and animals and old people are not killed by cars and trucks because cars and trucks are not necessary for travel. For short distances, the people fly; for longer distances they sit and meditate and then (as Meg Murry would say) they *tesser*, and they are there.

Is that more far-fetched than children in England growing new fingers? Not really. When Jesus wanted to go somewhere he didn't summon a taxi to take him to the airport. He *went*. And if we examine the Gospels carefully, we discover that sometimes he went farther than even the fastest runner could go in that length of time. His sudden appearances and disappearances confused and frightened the disciples, leaving them to say, "What manner of man is this?" And after the Resurrection his appearances are even more puzzling; at one point he is seen by five hundred of the brethren, but not everybody; in John's Gospel the disciples have seen him twice, and yet when they go fishing and see him on the beach, they don't recognize him. It is even possible that he may have been seen in more than one place at the same time, being even less restricted by time and space than he had been during his mortal life. And never once in his post-Resurrection appearances was he recognized immediately. Mary knew him when he called her by name. And he was known in the breaking of bread, in the eating of a fish.

We were not meant to be any more restricted than Jesus was during his sojourn with us here on this earth. If we take seriously that during the time of his Incarnation he was truly man, truly human as we are, than anything he did in his lifetime is available to us, too.

Am I suggesting that we really ought to be able to walk upon water? That there are (and not just in fantasies) easier and faster ways to travel than by jet or car? Yes, I am. There are too many stories of mystics being able to move hundreds of miles through the power of contemplation for us to be able to toss them aside. Over and over again throughout the centuries we have made choices which were meant to free us, but which ultimately have limited and restricted us. But the artist has retained some of the freedom we have lost in the industrial dailiness of our living.

Our way of looking at the place of the earth in the heavens changed irrevocably when the first astronauts went to the moon. Standing on the lunar surface, they looked back and saw "earthrise"—and all their concepts of up and down, backwards and forwards, left and right, changed. Since there is, in space, neither up nor down, left nor right, here nor there, backwards nor forwards, we can either fall apart in terror of chaos or rejoice in the unity of the created universe. Just as Jesus knew a world of nonlinear time, so, too, he knew a world of nonlinear space.

Theologians, back in the sixties, tried to grapple with this by saying that God is not "up there," that heaven is not "up," and they listened in awe as Yuri Gagarin, the first Russian cosmonaut to go into space said that of course there is no God; he was out in space looking for God, and he didn't see him. (As I try to visualize the "God" Gagarin was looking for, all I can do is smile.)

We look into outer space, and because we cannot "see" a God we can touch, a God we can comprehend with our rational intellects, we invent new gods to take his place, all the little gods of technocracy, little gods who have eyes and see not, ears and hear not, hands and touch not, and who have nothing to say to us in the times of our deepest need.

Montaigne saw this and wrote, "O senseless man who cannot make a worm, and yet makes gods by dozens." We have been doing this for centuries, and perhaps only the coming of the Kingdom will stop this futile activity.

Nonlinear space/time is more easily understood by poets and saints than by reasonable folk. Back somewhere around the end of the eleventh century, Hildevert of Lavardin wrote:

God is over all things,
under all things,
outside all,
within, but not enclosed,
without, but not excluded,
above, but not raised up,
below, but not depressed,
wholly above, presiding,
wholly without, embracing,
wholly within, filling.

And that says all that needs saying.

When I am looking for theologians to stimulate my creativity, theologians who are contemporary enough to speak to these last years of our troubled century, I turn to the Byzantine and Cappadocian fathers of the early years of the Christian era, because their world was more like ours than the world of such great theologians as Niebuhr and Tillich and Bultmann, who were writing in the framework of a world which was basically pre–World War II, and definitely pre-the-splitting-of-the-atom. In the first few centuries A.D., Rome was breaking up; civilization was changing as radically as is our own; people were no longer able to live in the luxury they had become accustomed to, as the great aqueducts and water-heating systems broke down and the roads were no longer kept up. Such people as St. Chrysostom, Basil the Great, Gregory of Nyssa, and his brilliant sister, Macrina, were facing the same kind of change and challenge that we are, and from them I get great courage.

And when I try to find contemporary, twentieth-century mystics to help me in my own search for meditation and contemplation, I turn to the cellular biologists and astrophysicists, for they are dealing with the nature of being itself, and their questions are theological ones: What is the nature of time? of creation? of life? What is human creativity? What is our share in God's work?

In his letter to the people of Ephesus, Paul wrote, "Each of us has been given his gift, his due portion of Christ's bounty." To accept our gift means accepting our freedom. This involves a new understanding of time and space, the same understanding towards which the astrophysicists are struggling, that same understanding which Jesus was offering John and James and Peter on the mountain, despite their obtuseness. They didn't begin to understand this kind of freedom until after the mighty acts of the Crucifixion, the Resurrection, the Ascension, and Pentecost, the coming of the Spirit.

And the men and women to whom Jesus offered this gift were ordinary human beings, faulted and flawed, just like the rest of us. He gave his disciples no job descriptions; he did not disqualify Mary Magdalene because she had been afflicted with seven demons; he did not spend a lot of time looking for the most qualified people, the most adult. Instead, he chose people who were still childlike enough to leave the known comforts of the daily world, the security of their jobs, their reasonable way of life, to follow him.

For the past several generations we've forgotten what the psychologists call our *archaic understanding*, a willingness to know things in their deepest, most mythic sense. We're all born with archaic understanding, and I'd guess that the loss of it goes directly along with the loss of ourselves as creators.

But unless we are creators, we are not fully alive.

What do I mean by creators? Not only artists, whose acts of creation are the obvious ones of working with paint or clay or words. Creativity is a way of living life, no matter what our vocation or how we earn our living. Creativity is not limited to the arts or having some kind of important career. Several women have written to me to complain about *A Swiftly Tilting Planet*. They feel that I should not have allowed Meg Murry to give up a career by marrying Calvin, having children, and quietly helping her husband with his work behind the scenes. But if women are to be free to choose to pursue a career as well as marriage, they must also be free to choose the making of a home and the nurture of a family as their vocation; that was Meg's choice, and a free one, and it was as creative a choice as if she had gone on to get a Ph.D. in quantum mechanics.

Our freedom to be creators is far less limited than some people would think.

Long before Jung came up with his theories of archetypical understanding, William James wrote: "Our lives are like islands in the sea, or like trees in the forest, which co-mingle their roots in the darkness underground. Just so, there is a continuum of cosmic consciousness, against which our individuality builds but accidental fences, and into which our several minds plunge as into a mother sea or reservoir."

The creator is not afraid to leap over the "accidental fences" and to plunge into the deep waters of creation. There, once again, and in yet another way, we lose ourselves to find ourselves.

One of the many sad results of the Industrial Revolution was that we came to depend more than ever on the intellect and to ignore the intuition with its symbolic thinking. The creator, and the mystic, have tended more towards Platonism than Aristotelianism, and tend to be willing to accept Plato's "divine madness," with its four aspects of prophecy, healing, artistic creativity, and love.

These divine madnesses have been nearly lost in this century, and so we've lived almost entirely in the pragmatic, Cartesian world. I wonder if Descartes knew what he was doing when he wrote his famous *I think, therefore I am*, and subsequently, if not consequently, we began even more than before to equate ourselves with our conscious minds. *Cogito, ergo sum* nudges us on to depend solely on intellectual control, and if we insist on intellectual control we have to let go our archaic understanding and our high creativity, because keeping them means going along with all kinds of things we *can't* control.

And yet, ultimately, our underwater, intuitive selves are never really incompatible with the above-water, intellectual part of our wholeness. Part of Jesus' freedom came from the radical view of time which allowed him to speak with Moses and Elijah simultaneously, thus bursting through the limitations of time accepted by the intellect. Yet what he did is not at all inconsistent with what contemporary astrophysicists are discovering about the nature of time. Secularists have long tended to laugh away the story of "Sun, stand thou still upon Gibeon," but according to some new research, it now seems as though something actually did happen to the physical world at that time; the earth may have shifted slightly on its axis, and time would have been affected, and the sun for a moment may indeed have stood still.

For the astrophysicist as for the saint, *chronos* and *kairos* converge. Robert Jastrow in his book, *God and the Astronomers*, talks about the astronomers after all their questions, struggling up to a mountain peak and finding the theologians already there.

CHAPTER SIX

KEEPING THE CLOCK WOUND

Chronos: our wristwatch and alarm-clock time. *Kairos:* God's time, real time. Jesus took John and James and Peter up the mountain in ordinary, daily *chronos;* during the glory of the Transfiguration they were dwelling in *kairos.*

Chronology, as we know it, began with Creation. Time exists only where there is mass in motion. A certain amount of consternation has been caused among some scientists because our great radio telescopes are giving clues that indicate that this universe did have a beginning, when an unexplained and violent explosion of an incredibly dense ball of matter suddenly burst into the void. As it exploded and expanded, our galaxies and solar systems were formed, and the original explosion continues as the galaxies hurtle outward into unknown space. What our radio telescopes are picking up now are echoes of the sound of that primal explosion, so long ago that it is scarcely expressible numerically.

As the echoes of the beginning linger, so, too, all that we say moves outward in gradually diminishing but never-ending sound waves. One of the more delightful mysteries of sound came when the astronauts on one of our early spaceships heard a program of nostalgic music over their sound system and radioed NASA to thank whoever it was who had sent them the program. From NASA came the rather baffled reply that they had sent the astronauts no such program and knew nothing about it.

This phenomenon triggered a good deal of interest and research: who had beamed the music to the astronauts? What was its source? All the radio and TV programs all over the country at that day and hour were checked out, and none of them was responsible for the music the astronauts had so enjoyed. Further research. Could they all have imagined hearing a nonexistent program of old popular songs? Was it a kind of mass hallucination? It seemed highly unlikely. Research finally revealed that that particular program had been broadcast in the 1930s.

How do you explain it? You don't. Nor can you explain it away. It happened. And I give it the same kind of awed faith that I do the Annunciation or the Ascension: there is much that we cannot understand, but our lack of comprehension neither negates nor eliminates it.

We simply do not understand time. We know that a moving mass is necessary for the existence of time as we define it and that time had a beginning and will have an end. We know that mass and energy are interchangeable and that pure energy is freed from the restrictions of time. But even *chronos* varies from time zone to time zone. When I flew to Cyprus, I had to make a seven-hour adjustment. Even within the United States I have had cause to tell someone who phones me at midnight, "Hey, I am not in California, and it is not nine o'clock here."

In my grandfather's lifetime there was no standardization of time such as we're accustomed to today. Every locality set its own time, according to its own convenience; one village might be two or three hours different from another just a few miles away, and there was outrage at the violation of freedom when the time zones were made obligatory. I have to admit that a certain amount of consistency is practical and helpful. However, no matter how we systematize it, chronological time does not work out evenly in the long run. We base it on the movement of the earth as it turns on its axis and around the sun, and on the movement of the stars across the sky—but every two thousand years or so the astronomers all have to adjust their timepieces a few seconds.

In *chronos* we are restricted to this unevenness; in *chronos* we live most of our lives and watch our bodies growing older, our skin losing its elasticity, our energies their powers of duration. For most of us a watch is accurate enough so that we know when to get up, to go to work, to go to church, to meet a friend. But even though we now have a moderately consistent chronology according to our clocks, there is considerable variation in our interior clocks. How long is a toothache? How long is a wonderful time? Lewis Carroll expressed a profound truth when he had the Mad Hatter say, "If you knew time as well as I do, you wouldn't be talking about wasting *it*. It's *him*. . . . We quarrelled last March . . . and ever since that . . . he won't do a thing I ask."

Lewis Carroll was a storyteller, an artist, as well as a mathematician, and artists often have a more profound sense of what time is all about than do the scientists. There's a story of a small village (about the size of the village near Crosswicks) where lived an old clockmaker and repairer. When anything was wrong with any of the clocks or watches in the village, he was able to fix them, to get them working properly again. When he died, leaving no children and no apprentice, there was no one left in the village who could fix clocks. Soon various clocks and watches began to break down. Those which continued to run often lost or gained time, so they were of little use. A clock might strike midnight at three in the afternoon. So many of the villagers abandoned their timepieces.

One day a renowned clock maker and repairer came through the village, and the people crowded around him and begged him to fix their broken clocks and watches. He spent many hours looking at all the faulty timepieces, and at last he announced that he could repair only those whose owners had kept them wound, because they were the only ones which would be able to remember how to keep time.

So we must daily keep things wound: that is, we must pray when prayer seems dry as dust; we must write when we are physically tired, when our hearts are heavy, when our bodies are in pain.

We may not always be able to make our "clock" run correctly, but at least we can keep it wound so that it will not forget.

Since time was created, had a beginning, and will have an end, it is a creature with whom we can have understandings and misunderstandings. All artists know days when time collaborates with them and they can do more than they can do in one day. There are other days when they are equally diligent, and yet get little or nothing accomplished.

Perhaps one of the saddest things we can do is waste time, as Shakespeare knew when he had Richard the Second cry out, "I have wasted time, and now doth time waste me."

But *being* time is never wasted time. When we are *being*, not only are we collaborating with chronological time, but we are touching on *kairos* and are freed from the normal restrictions of time. In moments of mystical illumination we may experience, in a few chronological seconds, years of transfigured love.

Canon Tallis says that his secretary does not understand that when he is thinking, he is working: she thinks he is wasting time. But thinking time is not wasted time. There are some obvious time wasters, such as licentious living, drunkenness, adultery, all the things Paul warns us about. A more subtle time waster is being bored. Jesus was never bored. If we allow our "high creativity" to remain alive, we will never be bored. We can pray, standing in line at the supermarket. Or we can be lost in awe at all the people around us, their lives full of glory and tragedy, and suddenly we will have the beginnings of a painting, a story, a song.

Some random words from my seatmate as I was flying to Evansville, Indiana, gave me the idea for a sort-of-science-fiction story: we see more and more Japanese-made cars on our roads, and if the Japanese wanted to retaliate for the dropping of the atomic bomb, they could make cars to self-destruct after a certain span of time or number of miles, killing all the occupants. . . . I will never write this story; it was, however, practice in seeing story wherever I go, whatever I do.

Time is to be treasured, worked with, never ignored. As the astrophysicists understand time now, it is not like a river, flowing in one direction, but more like a tree, with great branches and smaller limbs and twigs which may make it possible for us to move from one branch to another, as did Jesus and Moses and Elijah, as did St. Andrew and St. Francis when they talked with each other in that light of love which transcends all restrictions of time.

Kairos. Real time. God's time. That time which breaks through *chronos* with a shock of joy, that time we do not recognize while we are experiencing it, but only afterwards, because *kairos* has nothing to do with chronological time. In *kairos* we are completely unself-conscious and yet paradoxically far more real than we can ever be when we are constantly checking our watches for chronological time. The saint in contemplation, lost (discovered) to self in the mind of God is in *kairos.* The artist at work is in *kairos.* The child at play, totally thrown outside himself in the game, be it building a sandcastle or making a daisy chain, is in *kairos.* In *kairos* we become what we are called to be as human beings, co-creators with God, touching on the wonder of creation. This calling should not be limited to artists—or saints—but it is a fearful calling. *Mana,* taboo. It can destroy as well as bring into being.

In *Our Town,* after Emily has died in childbirth, Thornton Wilder has her ask the stage manager if she can return home to relive just one day. Reluctantly he allows her to do so. And she is torn by the beauty of the ordinary and by our lack of awareness of it. She cries out to her mother, "Mama, just look at me one minute as though you really saw me . . . it goes so fast we don't have time to look at one another." And she goes back to the graveyard and the quiet company of the others lying there, and she asks the stage manager, "Do any human beings ever realize life while they live it?" And he sighs and says, "No. The saints and poets, maybe. They do some."

Poets and saints. What an odd coupling. And yet

Freud, too, puts them together, saying that they are the two classes of human beings who defy all his psychological categorizing, who are full of surprises. Are we willing and able to be surprised?

If we are to be aware of life while we are living it, we must have the courage to relinquish our hard-earned control of ourselves. Because our reflexes have been conditioned as thoroughly as those of Pavlov's dog, this is never easy. But reflexes can be unlearned, or reconditioned. When my husband was on Broadway we were, perforce, night people, going to bed in the small hours of the morning and sleeping late. Now that Hugh is on a daytime television show, we have had to recondition our reflexes to become morning people, getting up early and changing our bedtime, too. It wasn't easy, but we made the transition, and now I find it difficult not to wilt around ten in the evening.

Daylight at first can be shocking and painful to the night-conditioned; it hurts the eyes, burns the skin; it takes a while to want it. And once we decide that we want the light, we must learn to trust it. We are given hints along the way, our nighttime dreams for one.

In our dreams we are bound neither by time nor space. We move through the ages and all over the world and sometimes beyond. In dreams we are able to fly, and though the Freudian frame of mind would label this as a mere sex symbol, I believe that it is far more than that, that it is a remembering of how we are meant to be.

I have always enjoyed my dreams and can remember clearly some that go back as far as my eighth or ninth year. I am often someone else in my dreams; I was once, when I was around eleven, an Elizabethan pirate. I am often not present in my dreams at all, not even as a conscious observer. Sometimes I dream full stories, and they are so satisfying as dreams that I seldom have any desire to put them on paper. Only very occasionally does something that comes to me in a dream end up in whatever it is that I am currently writing.

I do not want to become faddy about dreams, though I took them seriously long before it was popular to record them. If I wake up in the middle of the night with a dream which interests me, I do not turn on the light and write it down, which would stop me from sleeping for several more hours. I turn over and go back to sleep. If I'm meant to remember the dream in the morning, I will. I try to think about those I remember, to see if I may find in them some message from God which I was too stupid to understand during my waking hours.

Scripture is full of dreams; Joseph was no exception. And God often called people when they were asleep (Samuel, for instance) because in sleep we have let down our defense mechanisms. Pilate's wife, Claudia, told him not to execute Jesus because she had been warned about him in a dream, and I often wonder if he regretted not listening to her. Peter thought he was dreaming when the angels unlocked the gates and led him out of prison. If we are close to our angels, the dream world and the waking world will not be far apart.

In the creative act we can experience the same freedom we know in dreams. This happens as I write a story. I am bound by neither time nor space. I *know* those distant galaxies to which Meg Murry went with Charles Wallace and Calvin. I live in seventeenth-century Portugal with Mariana Alcoforado. But this freedom comes only when, as in a dream, I do not feel that I have to dictate and control what happens. I dream, sometimes, that I am in a beautiful white city I have never seen in "real" life, but I believe in it. I also believe in the planet Uriel, with its beautiful flying creatures, and also in that other planet where are found the unicorn hatching-grounds.

When we are writing or painting or composing, we are, during the time of creativity, freed from normal restrictions and opened to a wider world, where colours are brighter, sounds clearer, and people more wondrously complex than we normally realize.

Small children, knowing this freedom, do things which, to adults living in the grown-up world, are impossible. They see things which grown-up eyes cannot see. They hear things which fall on deaf ears with their parents. And they believe the things they do and see and hear. And when, eager and unprepared, they describe these marvellous things, they are told, by kindly and reasonable and well-meaning parents, that they have vivid imaginations. Less understanding adults tell the children that whatever it is they think they have done or seen or heard is impossible. Some children are told to stop telling lies. Some are even punished.

We grow up and forget. Peter didn't remember that he had forgotten how to walk on water, and so he walked—until he remembered—and then he got frightened and sank, and Jesus took him by the hand and pulled him out of the water and told him that he lacked faith.

Children are taught fear early: fear of water, fear of fire. Not that parents aren't right to warn; too many little ones have drowned, have been burned, because of careless parents. But there's a fine line between essential prudence for the child's sake and the destruction of creativity. Allowing the child a certain amount of solitude in a reasonably safe environment (no environment in this world is totally safe) is allowing the child's imagination to grow and develop, so that the child may ultimately learn how to be mature. Traherne says, "We do not ignore maturity. Maturity consists in *not* losing the past while fully living in the present with a prudent awareness of the possibilities of the future."

I was lucky as a child in being given a lot of solitude. Some of this was happenstance because of my father's illness and my lack of siblings. But it did provide me with an atmosphere in which imagination could flourish. And nobody told me it was childish to believe in angels. And so I was able to do a few impossible things.

For instance: when I was a small child, visiting my grandmother at her beach cottage, I used to go down the winding stairs without touching them. This was a special joy to me. I think I went up the regular way, but I came down without touching.

Perhaps it was because I was so used to thinking things over in solitude that it never occurred to me to tell anybody about this marvellous thing, and because I never told it, nobody told me it was impossible.

When I was twelve we went to Europe to live, hoping the air of the Alps might help my father's lungs. I was fourteen when we returned, and went to stay with my grandmother at the beach. The first thing I did when I found myself alone was to go to the top of the stairs. And I could no longer go down them without touching. I had forgotten how.

Did I, in fact, ever go down those winding stairs without touching them? I am convinced that I did. And during the years enough people have timidly told me of "impossible" things they have done that I am convinced that the impossible is open to far more people than we realize—mostly because we are fearful of being ridiculed if we talk about it. Ridicule is a terrible witherer of the flower of the imagination. It binds us where we should be free.

Freedom is a terrible gift, and the theory behind all dictatorships is that "the people" do not want freedom. They want bread and circuses. They want workman's compensation and fringe benefits and TV. Give up your free will, give up your freedom to make choices, listen to the expert, and you will have three cars in your garage, steak on the table, and you will no longer have to suffer the agony of choice.

Choice is an essential ingredient of fiction and

drama. A protagonist must not simply be acted upon, he must act, by making a choice, a decision to do this rather than that. A series of mistaken choices throughout the centuries has brought us to a restricted way of life in which we have less freedom than we are meant to have, and so we have a sense of powerlessness and frustration which comes from our inability to change the many terrible things happening on our planet.

All the Faust stories are studies in the results of choice. Dostoyevsky's story of the Grand Inquisitor in *The Brothers Karamazov* is one of the most brilliant pieces of Christian writing that I know, and one of the most frightening, because the Grand Inquisitor, like many dictators, is plausible; he wants people to be happy; he does not want them to suffer; the church, because of the great love it has for humanity, has done its best to reverse all the damage caused by Jesus, with his terrible promise of the truth that will make us free. We do not want to be free, the Grand Inquisitor assures Jesus. We want these stones to be turned into bread.

Why would God give the gift of freedom to creatures who are not ready for it, who have kept making wrong choices for thousands and thousands of years—ever since Eve listened to the snake? Freedom is a mistake, we might well agree with the Grand Inquisitor as we drive through the slums of any of our great cities, where buildings are gutted by tenants who are so frustrated by lack of heat in winter, no hot water ever, and sometimes no water at all, that they resort to burning the buildings in order to get relocated. Or buildings gutted by landlords (not *all* landlords are vicious and greedy) who cannot afford to heat them at the present price of oil or to keep the water hot, and in desperation burn the building for the insurance money and get out. If all our freedom has done is build up our financially bankrupt, corrupt, tottering cities, what good is it?

Neither philosophy nor theology help me much here. The painters and writers who see the abuse and misuse of freedom and cry out for justice for the helpless poor, the defenseless old, give me more hope; as long as anybody cares, all is not lost. As long as anybody cares, it may be possible for something to be done about it; there are still choices open to us; all doors are not closed. As long as anybody cares it is an icon of God's caring, and we know that the light is stronger than the dark.

I am encouraged by the young people who express their caring by giving several years of their lives to the Peace Corps or Vista or Food for the Hungry, who shun shoddy workmanship, who are building their own furniture, making pottery, doing needlework in a striving for that excellence we have lost by some of our choices.

I do not decry all that technology has given us. In the "olden days" I would have died in childbirth with both Josephine and Bion, and I am glad to be here in this alarming and disastrous and marvellous world. Western civilization may be on the decline, but a civilization which has produced Bach and Rembrandt and Dostoyevsky (to limit myself to three favourites) cannot be tossed aside as worthless.

Bach, who, in terms of the evolutionary process,

is as close to us in time as last night—Bach will always pull me back and give me the courage to accept that what our free will is meant to do is to help God to write the story.

What if?

What if—the basis of all story. The small child asks all the what ifs. All of life is story, story unravelling and revealing meaning. Despite our inability to control circumstances, we are given the gift of being free to respond to them in our own way, creatively or destructively. As far as we know, even the higher animals (with the exception, perhaps, of the dolphin) do not have this consciousness, not necessarily self-consciousness, but consciousness of having a part in the story.

And the story involves what seems to the closed mind to be impossible—another reason for disbelieving it. But, as Christians, we may choose to live by most glorious impossibles. Or not to live, which is why in the churches, by and large, the impossibles, the Annunciation and the Transfiguration and walkings on water and raisings from the dead, are ignored or glossed over.

I see my young friends groping back towards a less restricted view of time and space, though sometimes in frighteningly faddish ways. True contemplation is sought through drugs, which can never produce it. Séances and trips in the astral body are on the increase, and the church condemns and draws back. But if we do not offer a groping generation the real thing, they will look for it elsewhere, or they will fall, as George Tyrrell observed, for the garbage of any superstition.

It is not easy for me to be a Christian, to believe twenty-four hours a day all that I want to believe. I stray, and then my stories pull me back if I listen to them carefully. I have often been asked if my Christianity affects my stories, and surely it is the other way around; my stories affect my Christianity, restore me, shake me by the scruff of the neck, and pull this straying sinner into an awed faith.

CHAPTER SEVEN

NAMES AND LABELS

Remembering the lovely things we have forgotten is one of the reasons for all art. Surely the customs officer Rousseau *knew* those jungles he painted. And Marlowe, having Satan cry out,

Why, this is hell, nor am I out of it!
Think'st thou that I, who saw the face of God,
And tasted the eternal joys of Heaven
Am not tormented with ten thousand hells
In being depriv'd of everlasting bliss?

knew hell himself, for we know the terrible things as well as the beautiful. Bach, setting down the soprano and alto duet in the 78th Cantata knew such heavenly joy that it is shared by all who hear the music. In the act of creation our logical, prove-it-to-me minds relax; we begin to understand anew all that we understood as children, when we saw wee folk under the leaves or walked down the stairs without touching. But this understanding is—or should be—greater than the child's because we understand in the light of all that we have learned and experienced in growing up.

George Eliot says, "If we had a keen vision of all ordinary human life, it would be like hearing the grass grow or the squirrel's heart beat, and we should die of the roar which lies on the other side of silence. As it is, the quickest of us walk about well-wadded with stupidity."

Despite this wadding, the artist in the moment of creation does hear the tiny beating of the squirrel heart and does indeed die to self on the other side of silence, where he retains the vision which includes angels and dragons and unicorns. The great artists never lose this quality which the world would limit to children. And along with this "wadding with stupidity" comes the denigration of children's books and the writers of children's books. A year or so before she invited me to come to the conference on Ayia Napa, Dr. Marion van Horne asked me to give a talk on Christian children's books. A large part of my job was to give a definition of what, in fact, makes a Christian children's book.

Such a definition would seem to be a simple task, but it is not. It used to be answered the easy way: how many times is Jesus mentioned? But that doesn't work. Jesus may be mentioned on every page in a book that is neither for children nor Christian. It perturbs me to observe in how many contemporary novels "Oh, Christ!" and "Je*sus!*" are spattered over the pages, side by side with the four-letter words.

So the use of the name of Jesus is no criterion. And the fact that "Christian" stories are still *story* further complicates things, for story touches on the realm of art, and art itself is looked on as something unfit for the real world. There's another *New Yorker* cartoon that shows a woman opening the door of her house to a friend. We look through the door, and in the back of the house a man is writing at a typewriter, with a large manuscript piled on the desk beside him. The friend asks, "Has your husband found a job yet? Or is he still writing?"

A successful businesswoman had the temerity to ask me about my royalties, just at the time when my books were at last making reasonable earnings. When told, she was duly impressed and remarked, "And to think, most people would have had to work so hard for that." I choked over my tea, not wanting to laugh in her face.

A young friend of mine was asked what she did, and when she replied that she was a poet, the inquirer responded, amused, "Oh, I didn't mean your *hobby.*"

So it is not only the church that fobs off art as untrue or unreal, and art for children is the most looked-down-on of all.

Whether a story is to be marketed for grownups or for children, the writer writes for himself, out of his own need, otherwise the story will lack reality. There is no topic which is of itself taboo; if it springs from the writer's need to understand life and all its vagaries and vicissitudes, if it is totally honest and unself-pitying, then it will have the valid ring of truth. If it is written because it is what is at the moment fashionable, and not out of the writer's need, then it is apt to be unbelievable, and what is unbelievable can often be shocking and even pornographic—and this includes some recent children's books.

The world wants to shove us into what it considers the appropriate pigeonhole. I do not like to be labelled as a "Christian children's writer" because I fear that this will shove me even further into the pigeonhole which began to be prepared for me when *A Wrinkle in Time* won the Newbery medal. If I am so labelled, then the implication is that I am to be read only by children, and Christian children at that. Though the chief reason that *Wrinkle* was rejected for over two years and by thirty-odd publishers was because it is a difficult book for many adults, the decision was made to market it as a children's book; it won a medal for children's books. Therefore, I am a children's writer, and that is all I'm allowed to be.

But I'm a writer. That's enough of a definition. (I infinitely prefer to say that I am a Christian than to mention any denomination, for such pigeonholing is fragmenting, in religion as in art.) So. I am a Christian. I am a writer. When I am grappling with ideas which are radical enough to upset grownups, then I am likely to put these ideas into a story which will be marketed for children because children understand what their parents have rejected and forgotten. Because I am a struggling human being; trying to make sense out of the mean-inglessness of much of life in this century and daily searching for revelatory truth in Scripture, it's highly unlikely that I'll ever want to write novels of pessimism or porno, no matter how realistic my work. But I don't want to be shut in, labelled, the key turned, so that I am not able to grow and develop, as a Christian, as a writer. I want that freedom which is a large part of the Christian promise, and I don't want any kind of label to diminish that freedom. It is sad and ironic to have to admit that it does.

To write a story is an act of Naming; in reading about a protagonist I can grow along with, I myself am more named. And we live in a world which would reduce us to our social-security numbers. Area codes, zip codes, credit-card codes, all take precedence over our names. Our signatures already mean so little that it wouldn't be a surprise if, by the year 2000, we, like prisoners, are known only by our numbers.

But that is not how it was meant to be. Coleridge writes,

The Jews would not willingly tread upon the smallest piece of paper in their way, but took it up; for possibly, said they, the name of God may be upon it. Though there was a little superstition in this, yet truly there is nothing but good religion in it, if we apply it to man. Trample not on any; there may be some work of grace there, that thou knowest not of. The name of God may be written upon that soul thou treadest on; it may be a soul that Christ thought so much of as to give his precious blood for it; therefore, despise it not.

The name of God is so aweful, so unpronounceable, that it has never been used by any of his creatures. Indeed, it is said that if, inadvertently, the great and terrible name of God should be spoken, the universe would explode. The letters *JHWH* are a jumble of Hebrew consonants, and a better translation than "Jehovah" is "The Lord."

But we, the creatures, are named, and our names are part of our wholeness. It used to be a moment of great importance when someone said, "Oh, don't call me Mrs. X. Call me Anne—or Katherine. Alex or John. My name is a gift which I offer to you."

Now the name is taken automatically—grabbed away. On television programs, the interviewer immediately calls whoever he is interviewing—head of state, composer, scientist—by the first name.

I love the rare moments when I am permitted to offer my name to someone. And I love the letters which begin "Dear Madeleine," because the writers feel that I have already given the gift of the name through the books. And I remember times when I have been given a name—and to be given a name is an act of intimacy as powerful as any act of love.

A French priest, conducting a retreat, said,

To love anyone is to hope in him always. From the moment at which we begin to judge anyone, to limit our confidence in him, from the moment at which we identify [pigeonhole] him, and so reduce him to that, we cease to love him, and he ceases to be able to become better. We must dare to love in a world that does not know how to love.

We are to be children of the light, and we are meant to walk in the light, and we have been groping along in the darkness. The creative act helps us to emerge into the light, that awful light which the disciples saw on the Mount of Transfiguration, and which the Hebrew children saw on the face of Moses when he had been talking with God on Mount Sinai.

If we are blind and foolish, so were the disciples. They simply failed to understand what the light was about—these three disciples who were closest to him. They wanted to trap Jesus, Elijah, and Moses in tabernacles, tame them, pigeonhole and label them, as all of us human beings have continued to do ever since.

It seems that more than ever the compulsion today is to identify, to reduce someone to what is on the label. To identify is to control, to limit. To love is to call by name and so open the wide gates of creativity. But we forget names and turn to labels; there are many familiar ones today, such as:

Fairy tales are not real and should be outgrown. Christians are people who are not strong enough to do it alone.

Bach is mathematical; therefore he does not write with emotion.

Chopin is only a romantic.

El Greco must have had astigmatism to account for his elongated people.

All Victorian poets had TB.

Roman Catholics are not Christians.

Protestants cannot understand Holy Communion.

People who write for children are second-class and cannot write for adults.

And the list could go on and on and on. . . .

If we are pigeon-holed and labeled we are un-named.

Last spring I was briefly in Jerusalem as the guest of the publishers who were bringing out a book of illustrations of the Old Testament by children all over the world, wonderful people who asked me to write the text to go with the pictures, and who knew me by name. During my stay, in which I was driven about the countryside to see as many Old Testament sites and sights as possible, I was entirely within the Jewish community. To my surprise, several times I heard, in times of stress or irritation, "Oh, Christ!"

So, I repeat, the number of times the name of Jesus is invoked has little or nothing to do with whether or not a book is Christian. But before I struggle further with what is or is not a Christian children's book, I think it's important to ask: What is a children's book?

Added to the assumption that if you don't have enough talent to write for adults, you might try writing a book for children, is the further insult that if you really work hard and discover that you have more talent than you thought you had, you might advance enough to write a book for adults.

If you are not good enough to write a book for adults, you are certainly not good enough to write a book for children. I had written and published several "regular" novels before I dared try my hand at a children's novel. (I say "regular" novel because I was gently told by a friend that today the word *adult* in front of *novel* means porno.)

And that's just another example of pigeonholing.

Nancy Berkowitz, long a great friend of children's books and their writers, told me last year that I'd given her the best definition of a children's book that she'd heard. Having completely forgotten ever giving such a definition, I asked eagerly, "What was it?"

"A children's book is any book a child will read."

First my children and now my grandchildren are proof of this, moving from children's books marketed for their own age range—the girls are ten and eleven years old—to any grown-up novel I think would appeal to them. All they require is a protagonist with whom they can identify (and they prefer the protagonist to be older than they are), an adventure to make them turn the pages, and the making of a decision on the part of the protagonist. We name ourselves by the choices we make, and we can help in our own naming by living through the choices, right and wrong, of the heroes and heroines whose stories we read.

To name is to love. To be Named is to be loved. So in a very true sense the great works which help us to be more named also love us and help us to love.

One summer I taught a class in techniques of fiction at a midwestern university. About half way through the course, one of the students came up to me after class and said, "I do hope you're going to teach us something about writing for children. That's really why I'm taking this course."

"What have I been teaching you?"

"Well—writing."

"Don't you write when you write for children?"

"Well—but isn't it different?"

No, it is not different. The techniques of fiction are the techniques of fiction. They hold as true for Beatrix Potter as they do for Fyodor Dostoyevsky. Characterization, style, theme, are as important in a children's book as in a novel for grownups. Taste, as always, will differ (spinach vs. beets again). A child is not likely to identify with the characters in Faulkner's *Sanctuary*. Books like *A Wrinkle in Time* may seem too difficult to some parents. But if a book is not good enough for a grownup, it is not good enough for a child.

So what, then, are the differences?

Most of them are minor, and apparent. A child wants to read about another child, a child living in and having adventures in a world which can be recognized and accepted. As long as what the protagonist does is true, this world can be unlimited, for a child can identify with a hero in ancient Britain, darkest Africa, or the year two thousand and ninety-three.

When I was a child I browsed through my parents' books when I had finished my own. What was not part of my own circumference of comprehension I simply skipped; sex scenes when I was eight or nine had little relevance for me, so I skipped over them. They didn't hurt me because they had no meaning for me. In a book which is going to be marketed for children it is usually better to write within the child's frame of reference, but there is no subject which should, in itself, be taboo. If it is essential for the development of the child protagonist, there is nothing which may not be included. It is *how* it is included which makes its presence permissible or impermissible. Some books about—for instance—child abuse are important and deeply moving; others may be little more than a form of infant porno.

Children don't like antiheroes. Neither do I. I don't think many people do, despite the proliferation of novels in the past few decades with antiheroes for protagonists. I think we all want to be able to identify with the major character in a book—to live, suffer, dream, and grow through vicarious experience. I need to be able to admire the protagonist despite his faults and so be given a glimpse of my own potential. There have been a few young-adult novels written recently with antiheroes; from all reports they are not the books which are read and reread. We don't want to feel *less* when we have finished a book; we want to feel that new possibilities of being have been opened to us. We don't want to close a book with a sense that life is totally unfair and that there is no light in the darkness; we want to feel that we have been given illumination.

One summer at a writer's conference I felt that something was wrong with most of the juvenile manuscripts I received—not all of them, but enough so that it worried me, especially because I couldn't put my finger on what was wrong.

On the last day of the conference all the workshops were open, and almost everybody attended them all. Most of the students had been in two or three workshops, so I had the opportunity to listen to poems, stories, sections of novels, written by the men and women from my workshop. In almost every case, the work in the other workshops was better than the work they had turned in to me, and I discovered to my horror that they had been writing down, not so much down to children as down to themselves, writing below their own capacity. I listened to an excellent story written by a young man who had turned in some indifferent material to me, and after class I figuratively shook him as I said, *"That* is the way you write for children: the way you wrote that story, *not* the—junk you wrote for me."

A child is not afraid of new ideas, does not have to worry about the status quo or rocking the boat, is willing to sail into uncharted waters. Those tired old editors who had a hard time understanding *A Wrinkle in Time* assumed that children couldn't understand it either. Even when Farrar, Straus, & Giroux, to which house I am devoted, decided to risk taking it, they warned me that they did not expect it to sell well, and they did not think it could possibly be read by anyone under high school age. This is the typical underestimation of the adult as to the capacity of children to understand philosophical, scientific, and theological concepts. But there is no idea that is too difficult for children as long as it underlies a good story and quality writing.

As to *Wrinkle*, it reflects my discovery that higher math is easier than lower math, that higher math deals with ideas, asks questions which may not have single answers. My reading of Einstein, Planck, Dessauer, Eddington, Jeans, Heisenberg, etc., was for me an adventure in theology. I had been reading too many theologians, particularly German theologians. I was at a point in my life where my faith in God and the loving purposes of Creation was very insecure, and I wanted desperately to have my faith strengthened. If I could not believe in a God who truly cared about every atom and subatom of his creation, then life seemed hardly worth living. I asked questions, cosmic questions, and the German theologians answered them all—and they were questions which should not have been answered in such a finite, laboratory-proof manner. I read their rigid answers, and I thought sadly, *If I have to believe all this limiting of God, then I cannot be a Christian.* And I wanted to be one.

I had yet to learn the *faithfulness* of doubt. This is often assumed by the judgmental to be faith*less*ness, but it is not; it is a prerequisite for a living faith.

Francis Bacon writes in *De Augmentis*, "If we begin with certainties, we will end in doubt. But if we begin with doubts and bear them patiently, we may end in certainty."

The anonymous author of *The Cloud of Unknowing* writes, "By love God may be gotten and holden, but by thought or understanding, never."

Love, not answers.

Love, which trusts God so implicitly despite the cloud (and is not the cloud a sign of God?), that it is brave enough to ask questions, no matter how fearful.

It was the scientists, with their questions, their awed rapture at the glory of the created universe, who helped to convert me. In a sense, *A Wrinkle in Time* was my rebuttal to the German theologians. It was also my affirmation of a universe in which I could take note of all the evil and unfairness and horror and yet believe in a loving Creator. I thought of it, at that time, as probably a very heretical book, theologically speaking, which is a delightful little joke at my expense, because it is, I have been told, theologically a completely orthodox book. The Holy Spirit has a definite sense of humour.

I've finally discovered a way to make the point that writing is writing, whether the story is for the chronologically young or old. I give whatever group I am teaching two assignments. The first is to write an incident from their childhood or adolescence which was important to them. "Write in the first person. Nothing cosmic, just an incident. And do not write this for children. Repeat: *do not write this for children.* Write it for yourselves. Write it for each other."

When I am giving this assignment as part of a juvenile's workshop at a writer's conference, I will already have read the stories and chapters of books which the conferees have submitted. Thus far, in every case, the work they hand in for this assignment is better than the stories they wrote "for children."

I repeat, "But you don't write 'for children.' You write for yourselves. Do you understand how much better this work is than the story you submitted when you were writing 'for children'?"

The second assignment follows: "Rewrite this story, this time in the third person and from the point of view of someone else in it."

This is a useful assignment for teaching the beginning writer point of view, and it is not always easy. Often I get wails of, "But I can't!"

One eleventh grader in the class of techniques of fiction I teach at St. Hilda's and St. Hugh's School in New York, wrote a story of her move from the country to the city, to Harlem, when she was seven or eight years old. She was frightened by the tall buildings, the crowded streets, the constant noise of taxi horns and shouting and sirens. So she would escape to the park, where she found an old tree which had branches onto which she could climb. The tree became her friend, her confidante, her solace. At the end of the summer the tree was struck by lightning and felled. She had lost her best friend.

The tree and the child were the only characters in the story. When I gave the second assignment there was the expected, "I can't."

I gave her no hints. "You can. Use your imagination."

Her second story, written from the point of view of the tree, was much better than the first, and the class was delighted—and everyone had a glimpse of what imagination can do.

A Catholic priest at the Baptist, Green Lake Writer's Conference in Wisconsin, wrote a story about a man, a fly, and God. We switched the point of view to God in the second assignment and realized that this was a mistake; it would have been better for him to have tried the point of view of the fly.

I can't take credit for these assignments. They were given me by Leonard Ehrlich in the one "creative writing" class we were allowed in college. After graduation, when I went to New York and started sending the stories I had written during my four years at Smith around to various magazines, the result of this second assignment was one of the first to be sold.

From these assignments I will learn everything I need to know about the student's strengths and weaknesses in writing fiction and will have a good idea of where to go next in teaching techniques. I also learn a great deal about the students, which can in itself be helpful. So I gave these two assignments my first two days at Ayia Napa. Many of the eleventh and twelfth graders I teach in New York have had hard lives, come from broken families, have learned too early about anger and death and despair. But I had never read anything like the first assignments I had from the young men and women at Ayia Napa. Edith is married to a Kenyan and is becoming African, but she was born in the U.S. and schooled in an affluent suburb. One day the science teacher at her high school came to talk to the students about evolution. "I can prove we came from monkeys," he said. "Look at her." And he pointed at Edith.

Edith's second story, which she wrote from the point of view of the science teacher, was a lesson to me in Christian compassion. The teacher is forgiven, wholly forgiven, because she can look at that experience without feeling the hurt all over again.

Joseph, from Papua, New Guinea, wrote about his father's experience as a cook in the Australian army when Joseph was a child. One evening there were fifty extra men, and Joseph's father had not been told they were coming, and he didn't have enough food. So he was beaten by the Australians, and then boiling water was poured over him. The message of Joseph's story was love; it had not been easy for him to learn not to hate Australians, but he had learned. He is married to an Australian, and they have a charming baby. And he has taken hate and turned it to love.

And perhaps that is an essential ingredient of a Christian children's book (or any Christian book): the message of love. A Christian children's book must have an ultimately affirmative view of life.

So a children's book must be, first and foremost, a good book, a book with a young protagonist with whom the reader can identify, and a book which says *yes* to life. Granted, a number of young-adult books have been published with a negative view of life, just as with antiheroes. Again, from all I hear from librarians and teachers, they may be read once, but they are not returned to.

Not long ago a college senior asked if she could talk to me about being a Christian writer. If she wanted to write Christian fiction, how was she to go about it?

I told her that if she is truly and deeply a Christian, what she writes is going to be Christian, whether she mentions Jesus or not. And if she is not, in the most profound sense, Christian, then what she writes is not going to be Christian, no matter how many times she invokes the name of the Lord.

When another young woman told me that she wanted to be a novelist, that she wanted to write novels for Christian women, and asked me how was she to go about it, I wrote back, somewhat hesitantly, that I could not tell her because I do not write my books for either Christians or women. If I understand the gospel, it tells us that we are to spread the Good News to all four corners of the world, not limiting the giving of light to people who already have seen the light. If my stories are incomprehensible to Jews or Muslims or Taoists, then I have failed as a Christian writer. We draw people to Christ not by loudly discrediting what they believe, by telling them how wrong they are and how right we are, but by showing them a light that is so lovely that they want with all their hearts to know the source of it.

If our lives are truly "hid with Christ in God," the astounding thing is that this hiddenness is revealed in all that we do and say and write. What we are is going to be visible in our art, no matter how secular (on the surface) the subject may be. Some of those angry etchings of Hogarth, depicting the sordidness and squalor and immorality caused by the social inequities of his day are profoundly incarnational, for they are filled with anguished pity for the thief and the prostitute and the scum of the earth, and this compassion is Christ's.

When my mother was a little girl, there was a popular series of books about an appallingly pious little girl named Elsie Dinsmore. As I remember the story of one of these volumes, Elsie had a worldly papa whom she nevertheless adored and yearned to convert. One Sunday her papa had guests for lunch, and he asked her to play for them—something appealing and wicked by a composer such as Bach or Mozart. But on Sunday Elsie would play nothing but hymns. Papa insisted. Elsie refused. So she sat at the piano bench, martyrlike, refusing to soil her hands with secular music, until she fainted and hit her head. Then she had brain fever and nearly died, and papa was converted.

It is possible that in its day and age that book might have qualified as a Christian children's book. Much of it was familiar to my mother. When she was a child, children were not allowed secular music on Sunday, nor were they allowed to read secular books or play secular games. They had a game, much like Authors, which substituted Bible characters for authors, and with such diversions Mother and her numerous cousins always managed to have fun on Sundays—but there was none of the piosity which makes Elsie so unattractive and which limit her to her own setting and day. Sunday, no matter how differently we observe it in various times and places, is a day for remembering the Resurrection, and although we observe it with reverence, we also celebrate it with joy. Children are not reading the Elsie Dinsmore books today, but they *are* reading other stories by other writers of the same era.

I read my mother's copy of *The Secret Garden* by Frances Hodgson Burnett when I was a child. During a rainy weekend at Crosswicks I read it to a small group of eager little girls and, a generation later, to the children of some of those little girls, up in the attic bedroom as autumn winds shook the house. *The Secret Garden* is probably the most successful and most read and reread of Burnett's books; it is also Christian, though I don't remember whether or not it ever mentions Jesus. And it is more successful than *Little Lord Fauntleroy*, for instance, because it is a better piece of storytelling, less snobbish, and the message doesn't show, like a slip hanging below the hem of a dress. I think we can all recognize ourselves, at least to some degree, in Mary Lennox, who is as spoiled and self-centered a child as one can find, thoroughly nasty and unlovable, basically because she's never been taught to love anybody but herself. The secret garden is as much the garden of Mary's heart as it is the walled English garden, and we watch Mary's slow growth into the realization of other people's needs and then into love. Mary's journey into love is, in fact, her journey into Christ, though this is never said and does not need to be said.

E. Nesbitt was a nineteenth-century woman whose fantasy and family stories are still popular with children. It has sometimes been remarked upon as odd that she writes about warm and happy families when her own childhood was often lonely and full of traumas. But I think that's probably why she wrote about families, the kind of family she would have *liked* to have had. My own lonely childhood is very likely the reason why family is so important to me—my own present family of children and grandchildren and the families in my stories.

I probably didn't answer the young women who wrote to me about writing for Christians. Their chief job right now is to learn the techniques of fiction, to read as many of the great writers as possible, and to learn from them, without worrying about how often they went to church or to what denomination they belonged. The important thing to look for is whether or not they could *write*.

CHAPTER EIGHT

THE BOTTOM OF THE ICEBERG

I'm grateful that Bach's Christianity was realized in both his conscious and subconscious mind. But being a practising Christian is not part of the job description, and sometimes God chooses most peculiar people to be vessels of genius. My mother used to sigh because her beloved Wagner was such a nasty man. And I was horrified to have some students tell me that a lot of people actively disliked Robert Frost. How does one separate the art from the artist?

I don't think one does, and this poses a problem. How do we reconcile atheism, drunkenness, sexual immorality, with strong, beautiful poetry, angelic music, transfigured painting? We human beings don't, and that's all there is to it. Dostoyevsky's magnificent theology is not always compatible with his agonized life. Mozart wrote one of his merriest and most joyful pieces while he was frantic over his dying mother. Mendelssohn, who helped give Bach to the world, was a Jew.

It's all more than I can cope with—or, rather, it's more than my conscious mind can cope with. Jung says that we are far more than the part of ourselves we can know about and that one of the most crippling errors of twentieth-century culture has been our tendency to limit ourselves to our intellect.

We use only a fragment of our complex and superb brains, and we use this fragment oddly indeed. The right hemisphere of the brain controls the left side of the body and the intuition, we are told; and the left hemisphere of the brain controls the right side of the body and the intellect. And we're afraid of that left, intuitive side. *Left* in Latin is "sinister." In French, *left* is "gauche," "clumsy." When an English nobleman had a child out of wedlock, it was called "a child of the *left* hand." And politically the *left* is socialism or communism or anarchism. Odd.

Right. Intellect. In Latin *right* is "dexter"; the right hand is dexterous. Last summer while I was teaching at Mundelein College, one of the Sisters told me that a left-handed child had been upset on hearing that the *right* hand of God was the favoured place in heaven. In French, *right* is "droit," right on. Something correct or appropriate is called *right*. *Right* conduct, according to the *Concise Oxford English Dictionary*, is morally good. *Right*-mindedness is true, correct. (Do we ever call people left-minded?) People do things *right* side up as opposed to upside down. If you're on the *right* side of forty it means you're still in your thirties. If you're in your *right* mind, it means you aren't insane. Politically, the parties which lean towards conservatism or Nazism or fascism are to the *right*. Odd, again.

The poor old left gets left out.

When our son was four and in kindergarten he was taught that left is bad. He was naturally ambidexterous, and his teacher insisted that he use only his right hand, and put on his right shoe or boot first, because right is good, and left is bad. He didn't tell us of this until he was grown. It is an added horror that the woman who did this damage was the wife of a minister and considered herself a virtuous Christian woman.

Left is bad; art is bad; theatre is wicked; story is lie.

Left is *bad?*

When my mother broke her right arm, she discovered a talent for watercolour painting with her left hand. Whatever happened to make us fear the left so much that we call it bad?

From that misunderstood *left* come prayer and poetry and song, and these have a healing power we are losing touch with in this technocratic age.

One of the lecturers at Ayia Napa was Helen Mullen, a librarian from Philadelphia, who had us all in laughter or tears as she demonstrated her art of storytelling. One day she told us about visiting the pediatric wards of hospitals and telling stories to the children, many of whom were in severe pain. But while the children were listening to the stories, they did not feel the pain.

And I remembered my elder granddaughter's ninth summer, most of which was spent on the pediatric floor of a city hospital after she had been hit by a truck on her way home from swimming. She could not be given any painkillers because of the head injury, and she was in great pain.

As she returned to full consciousness, she said to her parents and grandparents, "I love you," and then, "Read to me." So we read to her, hour on hour. When our voices would tire and we would slow down, we would immediately hear, "Keep on reading," and so we kept on.

Story was painkiller, quite literally. When her brain was focused on story, then it was not on the pain center. Story was a more effective painkiller than any chemical medication.

Even the greatest neurologist knows little about the mysteries of the brain. But we would do well not to think of any part of it as *bad*.

Another oddity of the brain is that our eyes see upside down, and then our brain has to turn things *right* side up (and, maybe, *left* side up). I don't understand why we see upside down; I know that nobody has been able to make a camera that doesn't see upside down, and maybe there's a message for us in that. Maybe the job of the artist is to see through all of this strangeness to what really is, and that takes a lot of courage and a strong faith in the validity of the artistic vision even if there is not a conscious faith in God.

Left on!

That old iceberg analogy has become blunted from overuse and nearly destroyed by jargon, but it's still true: our conscious minds are indeed only the tiny tip of the iceberg which is above the water, and the largest part of ourselves is unseen below the water, below the conscious level, and it is not easy to admit this, to admit it and not fear that large part of ourselves over which we have very little control, but in which lies enormous freedom, and the world of poetry, music, and the region of that deepest and truest prayer which is beyond all our feeble and faltering words. We need the prayers of words, yes; the words are the path to contemplation; but the deepest communion with God is beyond words, on the other side of silence.

My son-in-law, Alan, says in his book, *Journey into Christ,* "Our identity is hidden, even from ourselves. . . . The doctrine that we are made after the image of God proclaims that the human being is fundamentally a mystery, a free spirit. The creative artist is one who carries within him the wound of transcendence. He is the sign that human beings are more than they are."

And, as St. Augustine of Hippo says, "If you think you understand, it isn't God."

Even when the artist bears the spirit (The Saint Matthew Passion; Michaelangelo's *Pièta; The Tempest)* he does not fully understand, and that is all right. The work understands. God understands. And God understands that part of us which is more than we think we are.

A real problem for most of us is that this "more than we think we are" is not necessarily recognized as good. It is difficult for most of us to recognize, accept, and affirm those large areas of ourselves which are not compatible with the image of ourselves we would like to project or which the world has taught us we ought to project. Jesus was very clear about these projections, referring to those who projected them as "whited sepulchres," clean and white without, and full of dead bones and decay within.

Part of our inheritance from our Puritan ancestors is a feeling that we "ought" to be good. Certainly it is not a bad thing to want to be good. The daily problem is that what my finite, conscious mind tells me I ought to do and what the untamed, submerged, larger part of me makes me do are often in direct conflict. But this is no surprise for the Christian. Two thousand years ago Paul of Tarsus admitted quite openly that the things he wanted to do were the very things he didn't do, and the things he didn't want to do were the very things he did. And yet Paul did not despair nor drop out. He was even able to accept the reality that he had cheered on the stoning of Stephen and had been one of the most successful persecutors of the early Christians. And yet when God took him by the scruff of the neck and shook him, he was able to let go, to let go of himself and his control of himself and instead trust God and experience a total reversal of his life. Alan Jones points out that before his conversion on the Damascus Road, Paul was suffering from *paranoia*, was out of his right mind. And afterwards he was in a state of *metanoia*—and metanoia means being turned around, repentance, being in a healthy state of mind.

A working out of the ambiguities of being good and caught in the traps of our own subconscious minds and the changes and chances of our most careful plans is present in all the books which speak most powerfully to me. A complete and unexpected change in the fortunes or destiny or path of the protagonist has always been an element of story-telling, from the most primitive to the most sophis-ticated. Cinderella never expected to leave the ashes of the fireplace and go to the ball in a gor-geous gown and glass slippers; Hamlet could not believe that the mother he adored had actually con-nived in the killing of the father he honoured; Nathanael did not believe that anything good could come out of Nazareth.

Reading about the response of people in stories, plays, poems, helps us to respond more coura-geously and openly at our own moments of turn-ing. If my faith falters, I may well give it a surge of renewal if I think of the story of Ananias and Paul. What faith Ananias must have had in what he could not control when he took blind Paul into his house and gave him his sight, with no guarantee that Paul had changed from the zealot persecutor. Neverthe-less, Ananias was daring enough to trust the mes-sage the Lord had sent him in a vision and to welcome Paul into his heart and home.

We don't hear much about visions nowadays. And yet they have always been an accepted part of life and literature. Hamlet was frightened by the ghost of his father, but not because seeing a ghost was considered impossible. Shakespeare takes it for granted that Caesar will take dreams seriously. The artist, by and large, is less afraid of the below-the-surface part of the personality, the messages of dreams, than (perhaps) the developer or the lawyer. But the general tenor of our age is scepticism and doubt. A casual scanning of Freud leads us to believe that everything in the subconscious mind is something nasty we have repressed, but perhaps it is the repression which has caused the nastiness, rather than whatever it is we have repressed. A lot of the time we don't want to know all of ourselves, our more ignoble motives, our greedy desires, our participations in the stonings of Stephens. But only if we accept all of ourselves, our flaws as well as our virtues (and we're all a grab-bag of good and evil, and by and large can't tell which is which) do we become useful servants—of our art, of our Lord.

Complicated creatures we are, aware of only the smallest fragment of ourselves; seeking good and yet far too often unable to tell the difference between right and wrong; misunderstanding each other and so blundering into the tragedies of warring nations, horrendous discrepancies between rich and poor, and the idiocy of a divided Christendom.

Sometimes I think that it is only laughter which saves us. George MacDonald says, "It is the Heart that is not yet sure of its God that is afraid to laugh in His presence."

If we are sure of our God we are free to laugh at ourselves, and artists have helped heal with laughter—from Molière's comedies poking fun at the human condition to Aristophanes' hilarity at our bewilderedly mixed emotions to some of Bach's mirth-filled and even slightly bawdy secular cantatas. It's all part of what helps keep us in proportion; we can best take ourselves seriously if we are free to laugh at ourselves and to enjoy the laughter of God and his angels. As William Temple remarked, "It is a great mistake to think that God is chiefly interested in religion."

When we take ourselves too seriously, as the chief or only object of God's interest, then we fail to understand the magnitude of his love and concern for us. Artist and saint alike grope in awe to comprehend the incomprehensible disproportion of the glory of God and the humility of the Incarnation: the Master of the Universe, become of the earth, earthy, in order to be one with his creatures so that we may be one with him.

In my Goody Book I've copied out some words which are important to me, but, alas, I do not know who wrote them:

> The saints (and artists) are those who not only accept, but rejoice in the incongruity and so learn that laughter is holy. The infinite disparity between God's love and man's deserts is an indubitable fact; the saint embraces it for joy. The greater the incongruity, the more wonderful the love and mercy of God. The saint does not call himself a worm because he enjoys being wormy, but because there is simply no other way graphic enough to express the richness of God and the meagreness of men. . . .

One night I woke up with the words of the twenty-second psalm in my mind, not the terrible words which Jesus cried from the cross, "My God, my God, why have you forsaken me," but the words, "I am a worm and no man," and instead of thinking elevated thoughts, I glimpsed a picture of Jonah sitting under his withered vine, furiously castigating the worm for eating his gourd, and then I heard the worm's disclaimer, "After all, I am a worm and no man," and laughing I went back to sleep, and that was the moment of gestation for the little play *The Journey with Jonah*.

I hope that I will never forget the salvific power of joyful laughter.

Each time an unexpected discovery is made in the world of knowledge, it shakes the religious establishment of the day. Now, we are often taught that it is unfaithful to question traditional religious beliefs, but I believe that we must question them continually—not God, not Christ, who are at the center of our lives as believers and creators—but what human beings say *about* God and *about* Christ; otherwise, like those of the church establishment of Galileo's day, we truly become God's frozen people. Galileo's discoveries did nothing whatsoever to change the nature of God; they threatened only man's rigid ideas of the nature of God. We must constantly be open to new revelation, which is another way of hearing God, with loving obedience.

The great artists keep us from frozenness, from smugness, from thinking that the truth is in us rather than in God, in Christ our Lord. They help us to know that we are often closer to God in our doubts than in our certainties, that it is all right to be like the small child who constantly asks: Why? Why? Why?

Caiaphas asked no whys. He was frozen into the rigidity of the religious establishment of Jesus' day, and because of this frozenness, he feared Jesus as a blasphemer. Throughout the ages, our religious establishments have on occasion followed Caiaphas rather than Jesus, and this is something we must be on the alert for, all of the time.

But how? How to stay open? How to make sure that the voice we hear is the voice of the Lord? There are all kinds of dirty devices that get in the way, a principal one being the climate of success in which we live, the need for success with our peers, in our careers, in our bank balances. The mistake is in thinking of the journey in terms of success at all (though inevitably we do). Success is one of the dirtiest temptations of the devil.

The great metaphysical poet, John Donne, writes, "To come to a doubt, and to a debatement of any religious duty, is the voice of God in our conscience: Would you know the truth? Doubt, and then you will inquire."

If my religion is true, it will stand up to all my questioning; there is no need to fear. But if it is not true, if it is man imposing strictures on God (as did the men of the Christian establishment of Galileo's day), then I want to be open to God, not to what man says about God. I want to be open to revelation, to new life, to new birth, to new light.

Revelation. Listening. Humility.

Remember—the root word of *humble* and *human* is the same: *humus: earth*. We are dust. We are created; it is God who made us and not we ourselves. But we were made to be co-creators with our maker.

I often seek theological insights in reading science fiction because this is a genre eminently suited to explorations of the nature of the Creator and creation. I'm never surprised when I discover that one of my favourite science-fiction writers is Christian because to think about worlds in other galaxies, other modes of being, is a theological enterprise.

What is this universe like? What are its possibilities? How deep is space? Why is there so much suffering? What does it mean? What if—

A long time ago I read a science-fiction story about a planet which earth was attempting to colonize, a harsh and unwelcoming planet with terrible weather and hostile inhabitants. Earth's best men and women were gathered into teams and sent to do the job, and expedition after expedition came home broken, failed. Finally the department head was changed. The new head did not look for the strongest and most qualified people he could choose. He went to the waterfronts, to the slums, and got together a contingent of thieves, prostitutes, indigents, and sent them. And where the able had failed, the disabled succeeded.

Why? For many reasons. First of all, they already had learned to survive in a hostile environment. Second, they had no place to go but up. Australia was largely colonized by outcasts from prisons. And the roll call of our first American pioneers was made up of people who needed, for one reason or another, to get away. The writer of science fiction—as all other fiction—draws on present knowledge and past history, and says: What if?

The *what if* always springs from what is known. The writer understands that it may take the mavericks rather than the beautiful people to overcome great odds because every work of art is the discovery of a new planet, and it may well be a hostile one. How dare the water say, "What if?" and, "Yes, but?" and see visions which threaten the status quo and do heretical things like Bach's putting the thumb under rather than over the other fingers on the keyboard and explore the vast underwater bulk of man's mind in the great unwieldly volumes of *Ulysses* and *Finnegan's Wake* and plumb the depths of human agony in *Crime and Punishment* or the wild paintings of Hieronymous Bosch?

The child, like the artist, asks, "Why?" and, "How?" and interrupts, "But—"

Schooling, instead of encouraging the asking of questions, too often discourages it. Edison was dropped from the public school system in second grade because he was considered uneducable (his mother, who believed in him, taught him at home). Einstein could not manage lower math; arithmetic was too hard for him, and he made mistakes in his equations, though his mind could rove through the universe, unfettered. Winston Churchill was an inept and unsuccessful schoolboy and young man. But, Why? the artist asks. And, What can be done about it? What are the possibilities? What if?

Honest, earnestly seeking doubt may well be part of the What if.

Many Soviet writers have grown up believing in their system, and only as they grew old enough to start serving their work did the work itself prod them into asking questions. Sinclair Lewis questioned whether or not we have been true to the American Dream in his satirical novels and in his more prophetic works, such as *It Can't Happen Here.* In the past decade we have had novels questioning the medical establishment, the political establishment, the religious establishment. Such works, if they are not scandal-mongering, are not anti-science, unpatriotic, nor heretical. They come from a longing that promised truth, that abundant life, which the present circumstances on our planet do not offer to more than a small minority of people, and which are too often rejected by those who could accept.

A help to me in working things out has been to keep an honest—as honest as the human being can be—unpublishable journal. Granted, much of my nonfiction work is lifted directly from my journals, but what I use is only a small fraction of these numerous, bulky volumes. If I can write things out I can see them, and they are not trapped within my own subjectivity. I have been keeping these notebooks of thoughts and questions and sometimes just garbage (which *needs* to be dumped some-where) since I was about nine, and they are, I think, my free psychiatrist's couch.

Not long ago someone I love said something which wounded me grievously, and I was desolate that this person could possibly have made such a comment to me.

So, in great pain, I crawled to my journal and wrote it all out in a great burst of self-pity. And when I had set it down, when I had it before me, I saw that something I myself had said had called forth the words which had hurt me so. It had, in fact, been my own fault. But I would never have seen it if I had not written it out.

Fiction, in a less direct way, will teach me, teach me things I would never learn had I not opened myself to them in story. And often the events of my life and the events in whatever book I am writing are so inextricably intertwined that I cannot sepa-rate them. But I always learn from the writing, and it is usually something unexpected; for instance, did I plan to study cellular biology before starting to write *A Wind in the Door*? Definitely not.

A third aid is to have someone to talk things over with, a friend, a minister or priest. It's usually a help if it's someone to whom we are not too close, to whom we are not biologically bound. I have a hunch that if we avail ourselves of all these aids we're not so likely to need a psychiatrist, for we have been helped to discover that truth which will make us free.

When I write things in my journal or open them up in story, I have to admit all the things that Freud saw in the subconscious mind, all kinds of unpleas-

ant things I'd rather not see in myself; but the subconscious mind can also be transformed, as Shakespeare realized when he had Ariel sing:

Full fathom five thy father lies.
Of his bones are coral made.
These be pearls which were his eyes.
Nothing of him that doth fade
But doth suffer a sea change
Into something rich and strange.

It is just as much a mistake to extol the subconscious mind at the expense of the conscious as vice
versa. A friend of ours took his small daughter to
a special collection at the Museum of Modern Art.
Many of the paintings seemed to be a spilling out
of all the glop in the artist's subconscious mind,
with no modification from the conscious level. Our
friend wondered if he was too square to understand
them, but his daughter was merely bored. It wasn't
that she couldn't understand modern art but that
she didn't like chaos untouched by cosmos. He
took her to the Guggenheim Museum, where she
loved Miró, Di Chirico, Braque.

In one of Ionesco's plays, *The Chairs*, an elderly
couple living on a small island spend the timespan
of the play waiting for the man who is going to
come to them with the message which will tell them
the meaning of life. As I remember the play (which
I saw a good many years ago) the old man and
woman keep shifting chairs about while the sharks
swim outside. At the very end of the play a man

comes on-stage, dressed in top hat and tails, and unrolls a script on which is written the meaning of life, and he mumbles: "Anhh, unhh, aunh . . ."

No. I won't accept that. That's chaos adding to chaos. Or am I misinterpreting? Is Ionesco saying that it is *hubris* to think that any human being can give one the key?

The art of the absurd can, indeed, be revelatory, as in Ionesco's *Rhinoceros,* which is an icon, an affirmation of the value of being fully human and so an affirmation of incarnation. But sometimes it can lead into madness, occasionally literal madness, as in the lives of Nijinsky, Nietsche, van Gogh. The boundary between Plato's divine madness and destructive insanity is so close as to be well-nigh invisible. It is frightening to have to accept the fact that much that has passed for art in this century has depicted distortion, meaninglessness, destructiveness. And it is interesting to note that when the art of the absurd was at its height, theologians began to announce the death of God. Religion and art both reflect what is happening to the world around us. And both must learn to discern the difference between revelation and nightmare.

Robert Lindner, author of *Rebel Without a Cause, The 50-Minute Hour,* etc., concludes in *Must We Conform?* that society today shows all the clinical symptoms of psychosis. This isn't the first time that a civilization has suffered from collective insanity, but one of the gravest dangers is the loss of the distinction between vision and delusion. Far too often today children are taught, both in school and at home, to equate truth with fact. If we can't understand something and dissect it with our conscious minds, then it isn't true. In our anxiety to limit ourselves to that which we can comprehend definitively, we are losing all that is above, beyond, below, through, past, over that small area encompassed by our conscious minds.

The result of this artificial limitation is rebellion. The destructive rebellion is the most apparent–the alarming rise in the number of juvenile delinquents, the school dropouts, the continuing dependence on drugs. But there is also constructive rebellion on the part of our kids, as in their rediscovery of fairy tale, fantasy, myth; needlework and stained glass and ceramics; dancing and singing and baroque music; surely their passion for the Pachelbel canon is a passion for order in a disordered world. And they love the combination of order and delight in a Bach fugue.

There is something healthily affirming about such structure, a promise that we have a part in the making of meaning. This is not a false promise or an unreal self-control but a promise that we are coauthors with God in the writing of our own story.

Laurens Van Der Post, writing about the Kalahari Bushman, says, "The extreme expression of his spirit was in his story. He was a wonderful story teller. The story was his most sacred possession. These people know what we do not: that without a story you have not got a nation, or a culture, or a civilization. Without a story of your own to live you haven't got a life of your own."

My children and their contemporaries, having grown up during the nightmare of the Vietnam War, where the story was ruthlessly taken out of their hands, are striving once more to return to the full health of living their own story and of thinking with their whole selves, affirming the left as well as the right.

But our story is never written in isolation. We do not act in a one-man play. We can do nothing that does not affect other people, no matter how loudly we say, "It's my own business." I think that our children are sensing this interdependence and that they would agree with James Baldwin that "the role of the artist is exactly the same as the role of the lover. If I love you, I have to make you conscious of the things you don't see."

There is much that we do not see, inequity as well as overfullness; the old woman groveling in the garbage can and the old man on the park bench remembering his first love; the woman who offers her coat to someone colder and the young man who snatches her purse. Good and bad in an incredible and seemingly inextricable muddle. Artists used not to be afraid to personify in order to simplify: Mr. Greatheart; Sir Toby Belch; Lady Teasle; Mrs. Do-as-you-would-be-done-by. Despite our efforts to label, we are often afraid to personify nowadays, because it means to call by name.

How many of us call the devil by name today? If we see God's love manifested for us in the Incarnation, the life and death and resurrection of Jesus, then we need to also recognize the malignant force that would try to destroy God's love in a particular way, too. The antagonist in a story or play is never vague or general; there is always a person behind the forces of evil; otherwise we will not take them seriously. Mephistopheles, without a name, would not be nearly so tempting, or horrifying.

I have a friend who is a fine writer, one of the best storytellers around, who goes regularly to A.A. Several times she remarked to me how much more spiritual sustenance she gets from her A.A. meetings than from church. When I asked her why, she replied, "In A.A., the enemy has a name."

The enemy has a name in church, too, but we've forgotten it. In the Bible it is usually Satan. The most poignant name to me is Lucifer because Lucifer means, literally translated, "light bearer." That loveliest of all angels, the light bearer, turned from God to self-will, and ever since Michael and his angels threw him out of heaven he has been walking to and fro on the earth, as the book of Job reminds us, seeing what he can do. Lucifer. What happened? How did he fall into the pit of pride?

Chesterton said that it was by gravity that Satan fell; one sees representations of the devil sneering, but never in a state of levity, merriment, joyous laughter.

I'm grateful once again that I went to my Bible stories with no preconceptions because many of them are hilarious. If I'm depressed or out of sorts with God and man, all I have to do is read the book of Jonah. And surely God was amused at some of his early conversations with Moses. "Who am I?" Moses asks. And God replies, "Certainly I will go with you." Many of the parables make sense only if we realize that Jesus was telling a funny story to make his point, a funny story that was supposed to be greeted with a laugh, like the story of the judge and the importunate widow. And what about exaggeration for effect? Jesus wasn't afraid of hyperbole. What about the camel going through the eye of the needle? Or the man with the beam in his own eye who sees the mote in his brother's? And people accuse *me* of exaggerating!

I've been doing my evening Scripture reading in the French *Jerusalem Bible,* and came, the other night, to the parable of Caesar's coin, and coming upon it afresh, its humour hit me, and I burst into laughter. French is the only language besides English in which I am even moderately conversant, but it helps us to regain newness if we can look at something in a tongue other than our native one. I struggle on occasion with bits of the Bible in Spanish, Latin, German. I've tried the 121st Psalm in Swedish and the 18th in Hebrew, and some of the Canticles in Greek. It's fun, and as long as one doesn't stumble over the block of perfectionism, it's not all that difficult.

We need to be careful about the difference between laughter which is healthy and creative and laughter which, like Satan's, is destructive—at someone else's expense. The laughter in the Bible is never nasty (for that kind of laughter isn't laughter at all) and true laughter is freeing. We can laugh with pleasure as Jesus holds out his hand with the Roman coin, turning away wrath with a soft answer, a smile: Render to Caesar what belongs to Caesar and to God what belongs to God.

I was outraged a number of years ago to read a

book by an eminent Freudian analyst whose theory was that all artists are neurotic, psychotic, sado-masochists, peeping Toms; that not one is normal.

At this moment I do not know why it bothered me so. He means one thing by his labels; I would call it something quite different; but there is no denying that the artist is someone who is full of questions, who cries them out in great angst, who discovers rainbow answers in the darkness and then rushes to canvas or paper. An artist is someone who cannot rest, who can never rest as long as there is one suffering creature in this world. Along with Plato's divine madness there is also divine discontent, a longing to find the melody in the discords of chaos, the rhyme in the cacophany, the surprised smile in time of stress or strain.

It is not that what *is* is not enough, for it is; it is that what *is* had been disarranged and is crying out to be put in place. Perhaps the artist longs to sleep well every night, to eat anything without indigestion, to feel no moral qualms, to turn off the television news and make a bologna sandwich after seeing the devastation and death caused by famine and drought and earthquake and flood. But the artist cannot manage this normalcy. Vision keeps breaking through and must find means of expression.

CHAPTER NINE

DO WE WANT THE CHILDREN TO SEE IT?

f to be in a healthy state of mind means to be whole (not divided into left and right), and if to be whole means to be holy, then wholeness is what the Christian artist seeks. It is what the Christian seeks. It is what any artist seeks.

A pianist does not have to be a practicing Christian to play Beethoven's Appassionata Sonata or the rippling second movement of Ginastera's piano concerto. As my friend Tallis once remarked, "When your car breaks down, you don't ask if the mechanic is an Episcopalian. You want to know how much he knows about cars."

I want my doctor to be well trained, to take the Hippocratic oath seriously; I don't need to know about my surgeon's sex life or his religious affiliation. So why should I care what Emily Brontë or Bracque or Vaughan Williams believed? But I do care. Perhaps if I knew my surgeon as well as I know the great artists who inspire me, I'd want to know more about what he believes, too. But why? What does it have to do with the skill with which the surgeon wields the knife? Or how Picasso painted or Madeleine Grey sang or William Blake wrote?

If we are whole, then it does have something to do with it, but that something may not be what we expect.

Is there, then, any difference in the creative process for the Christian and the non-Christian?

Yes. No.

There may be a great deal of difference in work which has no element of transcendence. Times Square and Eighth Avenue in New York, which used to have the glamour of serious theatre, are now filled with porno movies and massage parlours and head shops. Even an "art" movie is not likely to be good box office unless it has at least one gratuitous nude scene. It is not that the nude body cannot be art or that it cannot be seen, appropriately, on-stage. But porno cheapens the body by treating it as a thing, a thing to be used, controlled, manipulated, an object whose free will is of no importance.

We're not the only generation to seek titillation in perversion, though I doubt if it's ever been so open since the days of the great Roman excesses. Our civilizations are not dissimilar, both reflecting the end of something rather than looking towards a new beginning (which is always the stance of the artist), and both are the expressions of a secular culture, accepting only the immediate and shunning the transcendent.

We shudder at the thought of the Roman arenas, with masses of people getting a thrill out of seeing other people being torn to pieces by lions, by each other. But we, too, have burdens on our conscience.

These burdens are reflected in the work of many serious artists, even when the work seems to have little, on the surface, to do with current offenses against humanity. One can cry out in anguish against tortures in Chile, in Iran, by writing about a coyote hunt in Arizona. Human problems transcend their locale without losing any of their particularity.

An artist seeking for the truth behind human brutality may express it in the bleeding body of an animal shot for sport rather than need. The truth of an incident may lie artistically far from the facts of that incident. The most difficult part of trying to show truth lies not only in believing in it oneself but in making it believable to the reader, viewer, listener.

Credibility in creativity is a hard lesson to learn, and I'm grateful that it was pointed out to me early by Leonard Ehrlich, who gave me those useful first two assignments. I had written a story for him in fulfillment of an assignment, and when he returned it to me, he said, "It's well written, Madeleine, but I don't believe it."

"But it's true," I defended hotly. "I wrote it exactly the way it happened. It's true."

Calmly he replied, "If I don't believe it, it isn't true."

Like many lessons, that was painful. But I had to take it seriously. No matter how true I believe what I am writing to be, if the reader cannot also participate in that truth, then I have failed. I learned slowly, struggling to acquire the technique which will help me to become more able to put down on paper the truth I see. The artist seeks that truth which offers freedom and then tries to share this offering.

I am made more free by my participation in the work of other artists, especially the giants. And it is the other artists who teach the rest of us, offering their vision of truth.

And if this vision is true, how can it conflict with the truth which Christ told us to know?

It is one of those odd ironies that Anglican Madeleine is often asked to speak in Roman Catholic and Evangelical settings and seldom, until very recently, in Episcopal ones. The two colleges where I feel most at home, and where I have been going regularly for the past decade, are Mundelein, in Chicago, which is Roman Catholic, and Wheaton, less than an hour away, which is Evangelical. You'd think they'd be about as far apart as Christians can get, but I feel equally at home and befriended in both places. I do not change my voice; I do not need to translate into different theological languages; we are far closer than we realize. Especially when the topic is art, for art cuts across all denominational barriers. Art *is*.

Mundelein may be more familiar with sign and

symbol than Wheaton, but sign and symbol, sacrament and myth, metaphor and simile, are essential to all art, regardless of the personal belief or lack of belief of the artist.

In a lecture at Wheaton I quoted the Anglican theologian, H. A. Williams, *"The opposite of sin can only be faith, and never virtue."*

The creative process has a lot to do with faith and nothing to do with virtue, which may explain why so many artists are far from virtuous—are, indeed, great sinners. And yet, at the moment of creation, they must have complete faith, faith in their vision, faith in their work.

Again, the degree of talent, the size of the gift, is immaterial. All artists must listen, but not all hear great symphonies, see wide canvasses, conceive complex, character-filled novels. No matter, the creative act is the same, and it is an act of faith.

A ten-year-old boy asked me of *A Wrinkle in Time,* "Do you *believe* all that?"

"Yes," I replied. "Of course I do."

The artist, like the child, is a good believer. The depth and strength of the belief is reflected in the work; if the artist does not believe, then no one else will; no amount of technique will make the responder see truth in something the artist knows to be phony.

My faith in a loving Creator of the galaxies, so loving that the very hairs of my head are counted, is stronger in my work than in my life, and often it is the work that pulls me back from the precipice of faithlessness. It is not necessarily an unmixed blessing to be a well-educated person in a secular society. A man whose name is unknown to me but whose words I copied out years ago wrote, "God must be very great to have created a world which carries so many arguments against his existence."

To work on a book is for me very much the same thing as to pray. Both involve discipline. If the artist works only when he feels like it, he's not apt to build up much of a body of work. Inspiration far more often comes during the work than before it, because the largest part of the job of the artist is to listen to the work and to go where it tells him to go. Ultimately, when you are writing, you stop thinking and write what you hear.

To pray is to listen also, to move through my own chattering to God to that place where I can be silent and listen to what God may have to say. But if I pray only when I feel like it, God may choose not to speak. The greatest moments of prayer come in the midst of fumbling and faltering prayer rather than at the odd moment when one decides to try to turn to God.

We used to call my mother (usually collect) once a week; then, in her last years, several times a week, just to keep in touch. We, in our turn, like our children to keep in touch with us. If they never called, then they might be so far from our own busy lives that they might not even know if the phone number was changed.

A faltering analogy. But it is good for the children to keep in touch. It is good for all of us children to keep in touch with our Father.

Work. Prayer. As with all of life, it is a rhythm: tension, release; tension, release. Work, discipline, obedience; pull the bow string taut, and then let go. But it must be done daily.

I tried to talk about the necessity for both work and letting go in the creative process one hot morning at Ayia Napa. I learned long ago that the listener hears not always what is said but what he wants to hear.

The response to that particular morning's lecture made this problem especially clear. I had spent half the lecture on the necessity for discipline, regularity in work habits, obedience, and the other half on letting go our rigid self-control in order to listen to the work. After the lecture, two young men came up to me, both deeply troubled over what they had heard. Mitau, an Asian, who had won a prize for his first story and wanted a literary career handed to him on a silver platter, heard nothing but the injunctions to work. Discipline, he heard. "Write every day, whether you feel like it or not. Be obedient to the work. Work, work, work," was all he heard.

Julio, a South American minister who lives in a community filled with ecstatic charismatics, heard nothing but, "Don't think. Write."

"But you heard only half of what I said!" I told them and tried to make each hear the part he had ignored. The balance of tension and release is somewhat like that of a violin; the strings must be taut before they will play, but if they are not released, they will break.

Did I, in the end, get them to realize that each had heard only a selected part of what was said? I hope so. But I am not sure. For when I am reading or listening, I, too, tend to hear what applies to me, in my particular situation.

In psychology class in college I remember the professor telling us that if we suddenly become interested in, say, mitochondria, we will come across articles on mitochondria in newspapers and magazines; they will appear to be in the news everywhere. But, if it were not for our particular interest, we would not have noticed the articles or turned on the television programs.

I doubt if there's any such thing as total objectivity. We listen out of our own skins, our own ears, see through our own eyes with their various myopias and astigmatisms. A history of either the English or American Civil War will show a totally different war when told from the point of view of one side or the other. The villains of one book will be the protagonists of the other. The historian trying to show both points of view fairly is still caught within his own subjective interpretations. We come more closely to a clear view in the novels of Dostoyevsky, Robertson Davies, the plays of Shakespeare.

In an interview in a well-known Christian magazine, I explained earnestly that we are limited by our points of view; "I have a point of view," I told the interviewer. "You have a point of view. But *God* has *view*." When the article appeared, some over-diligent copy editor had changed it to, "I have a point of view. You have a point of view. God has a point of view."

I wrote back in a white heat. "This is a theological error. Please correct it. The *point is* . . ."

In our daily living the actions we choose, from within our own skins, as the best possible under the circumstances, may well turn out to have been the wrong ones. Something we regret at the time as abysmally stupid may well end up being the one thing needed under the circumstances. We are trapped in unknowing.

Nothing is certain. I sat writing on my first novel, quite bogged down, and in annoyance at my own lack of creativity got up and walked across the room. As I reached the window, the heavily molded plaster ceiling crashed down where I had just been sitting. My husband came home on the subway train just before the one that had the accident; someone else's husband didn't. On a calm and sunny summer afternoon someone came to tell my daughter and her husband that their little girl had been hit by a truck. A kind word twenty years ago may be responsible for an unexpected good job today.

Literature deals with this inability to see around the corner, and the disastrous results when we play at being God. The Macbeths could have refused to heed the witch's foreseeing that Macbeth would wear a crown. Beauty's sisters thought she was a stupid girl to honour their old father to such an extent that she gave herself to the terrible beast in his palace. How enraged these pragmatic sisters must have been when the beast turned out to be a handsome and wealthy prince, bewitched until someone should kiss him in spontaneous affection.

But Beauty could not know that her act of compassion would release the spell.

We don't know. We can only make guesses, and our guesses may be wrong. Far too often in this confused world we are faced with choices, *all* of which are wrong, and the only thing we can do, in fear and trembling, is to choose the least wrong, without pretending to ourselves that it is right. As I look at all the great protagonists of literature, from Greek drama to the contemporary novel, and add up the results of all the choices, and the motivation behind the choices, I keep coming back to that reason of my husband's for turning down a lead role in a cheap play:

Do we want the children to see it? That's as good a criterion as any I've found.

It is a criterion of love. In moments of decision, we are to try to make what seems to be the most loving, the most creative decision. We are not to play safe, to draw back out of fear. Love may well lead us into danger. It may lead us to die for our friend. In a day when we are taught to look for easy solutions, it is not always easy to hold on to that most difficult one of all, love.

During a summer session at Wheaton, one of the students asked, "Do you think there are any absolutes?"

I thought for a second and then said, off the top of my head, "Yes, I think the ten commandments are absolutes." Later, as I set them against the great works of literature, they seemed to hold fast. When we break one of the commandments, we are doing something we would not want the children to see. We are being destructive rather than creative. We are taking things into our own hands and playing God. Playing God, hubris, presumption, the tragic flow of all the great Greek heroes. But having broken the first commandment, it is almost inevitable that the breaking of others will follow. Oedipus dishonours both his parents. Anna Karenina commits adultery. Macbeth is covetous. Dorian Gray makes a graven image of himself. Iago bears false witness against his neighbour. And so it goes. Whenever the first commandment is broken, more breakage follows. We are, as a consequence, unable to love ourselves, and so we are not able to love our neighbour.

We take things into our own hands. We listen to promises of security, promises that can only be false. We forget those absolutes against which we can set our behaviour, make our decisions. And we lose heart and are no longer able to pluck out of the nettle danger, the flower of courage.

And we draw back.

At school in Charleston I was running, tripped, and fell through a window. I picked myself up in a shower of glass and did not have a scratch on me because I did not have time to draw back. If I had, I would have been cut, and badly.

Starting a novel demands a conscious falling *through* the window, a journey *through* the looking glass, and a return to the imaginative courage of the child.

Dare I? Of course I don't. But I'm going to anyhow because I have no choice.

How do we survive the unreliability of life in this world? Everything appears to be going along smoothly, and then, without warning, tragedy strikes.

I flew out to Chicago one July, to speak at Wheaton, and was met by a young graduate, a friend of mine. She took me to her home for a cup of tea, and I called my husband, who was at Crosswicks, as I always do after a trip, just to check in. And what I learned was that my just-nine-year-old granddaughter Léna had been hit by a truck on her way home from swimming. That was all he knew because to add to the unreliability of all things, our phone was out of order when I first called, and the operator reported it. During the fifteen minutes I waited before calling again, a neighbour had called him frantically for information. So it was she who told him what she knew: the little girl had been hit by a truck and was being taken from the local hospital to the bigger hospital in Hartford. We knew that this meant head injury because the local hospital could take care of everything except a neurological problem.

While we had been drinking tea, my young friend had informed me that she had decided not to marry and have children. She was a painter, and a fine one, and she felt that a family would interfere with her work. Still with my hand on the phone, I said slowly, "The decision you have made means that you will never have to go through the anguish I'm going through now. But I don't think I would want to be in a position where I could *not* know it."

She drove me to Wheaton, and I called home again. Our daughter having at last been able to reach her father, we now knew the terrifying extent of the damage. Both of Léna's femurs were broken, up near the hips. Her ribs were broken. Her jaw was broken in two places. Her skull was fractured. She had a head wound which laid bare the bone. Her arms and legs were covered with lacerations and contusions. Léna was the little girl whose pain we alleviated by reading stories hour after hour, so this is a story with a happy ending, but that evening we did not know what the ending was going to be. She was unconscious, and the neurosurgeons were pessimistic. Worse than the fear of death was the fear of terrible brain damage.

Because I was at a Christian college, I was able to ask my friends for prayers, and a network of prayer quickly went out. That evening, after my lecture, Mel Lorentzen stepped up to the lectern and told the audience what had happened and asked for prayers. And I went back to my room to try again to reach Canon Tallis in New York, and the Episcopal Sisters who ran the school where my little granddaughters had gone and from which their mother had graduated. I had not been able to get any calls through, and I could not understand why. Finally the phone at the convent began to ring, and it rang and rang, and I waited until it was answered by Mother Mary Christabel, who told me that she had had to grope to the phone in the darkness because New York had plunged into a blackout. I told her what had happened and asked for prayers. Then I got ready for bed, and part of my bedtime routine is to read Evening Prayer. I opened the small prayer book I bring with me when I travel, and when I came to the psalms for the evening, there was a picture of nine-year-old Léna, taken just a few weeks before, at the baptism of her baby brother. It was almost more than I could bear. I held the prayer book loosely, and a card fell out, a card given me years ago by one of the Sisters at Mundelein (how intricately the strands are woven). On it were the words of John of the Cross: "One act of thanksgiving made when things go wrong is worth a thousand when things go well."

And I knew that I had to make that act of thanksgiving.

I'm sure I was given the grace to make it that night and during the several days that followed, when I jammed many lectures and classes into a short time in order to be able to get home to the family as soon as possible. The largest part of that act of thanksgiving was gratitude for my children and grandchildren, for the first nine years of Léna's life, and then to say with Lady Julian of Norwich, "But all shall be well and all shall be well and all manner of thing shall be well," and then to add, "No matter what." That was the important part, the "no matter what."

It was ten days before Léna regained full consciousness and we knew that she would recover.

The gift of that card falling out of my prayer book when it did was one of the greatest gifts I have ever received. It made me affirm to myself that God is in control, no matter what, that ultimately all shall be well, no matter what.

That autumn Mother Mary Christabel told me that at the onset of the blackout their phone had gone dead; they hadn't even been able to use the inter-com between the convent and the school. They could make no calls out. No calls came in. Except mine, my plea for prayer.

Jacques Lusseyran, in *And There Was Light*, tells us that for the child, what happens is from God and is good. A child will never feel self-pity unless some adult is stupid enough to suggest it. And he reminds us that courage, which we grownups make so much of, is for the child the most natural thing in the world.

I saw the truth of those words as I watched Léna during that long summer, when she never once said, "Why did this happen to me?" or questioned the rightness or wrongness of her pain in any way. Not once did she whine; she screamed with pain; if anyone bumped the ropes which held her legs in traction, it caused her excruciating pain; but she didn't whine. And if I needed an example of calm courage, I found it in my daughter, who was nurs-ing a two-month-old baby and who kept on nursing with no loss of milk. We will always be grateful to the head nurse, who allowed us to bring the baby onto the pediatric floor, contrary to the regulations. When the student nurses came to that part of their training when they had to wash a baby, instead of using the usual doll they used Edward, who quickly became a great pet on the floor.

I have heard that in time of tragedy, a family either breaks apart or draws together. I will be eter-nally grateful that ours drew together. My son, who had planned to spend the summer at his university, writing, came home immediately to help out with the driving, the cooking, with whatever was needed.

His medical-student bride-to-be spent her one week of vacation with us, in order to make the hour-long daily drive to the hospital to see Léna. How much I learned from all of these people who are so close to me that sometimes I do not remember what they teach me. But the two deepest lessons were Léna's uncomplaining acceptance and her mother's loving courage.

It was a long summer, and a hard one, but there were many joyful times, and funny ones, too. Most of the children had little television sets, with hearing discs they could put under their pillows in order not to disturb the others, and we got one for Léna. One day one of the nurses who hadn't seen her since she had been in the Intensive Care Unit, came to visit. Léna was watching *All My Children* on television, and the nurse said, "What are you watching, Léna?" "I'm watching my grandfather." At that the nurse hurried to the nurses' station and said in great agitation, "The child's delirious!" There was much laughter as she was reassured that the little girl was indeed watching her grandfather, who plays the head of the hospital in that TV show.

All shall be well and all shall be well and all manner of thing shall be well. No matter what. That, I think, is the affirmation behind all art which can be called Christian. That is what brings cosmos out of chaos.

CHAPTER TEN

THE JOURNEY HOMEWARD

Light—dark; brilliance—cloud. How often God appears in a cloud. A cloud was the sign of God's presence as he led Moses and the children of Israel towards the Promised Land, and the cloud by day became a pillar of fire by night. The psalmist sings out the great affirmation, "Yes, the darkness is no darkness with you, O Lord, but the night is as clear as the day; the darkness and light to you are both alike."

A cloud covered Jesus and Moses and Elijah, that extraordinary cloud which signals God with Us. As Gregory of Nyssa points out, when Moses first talked with God, he talked in the light, but as he grew in spiritual stature he talked with God in the darkness. But what darkness! When Moses came down from the mountain his face shone with such brilliance that the people could not bear to look at him, and after that whenever he went into the darkness of the cloud to talk with God, he had to cover his face when he returned so that the brilliance of his countenance would not blind the people.

Perhaps it is only the artists who have not forgotten that cloud of brilliance which shines through all Scripture. Ezekiel knew it, with his great wheels of light. Adam and Eve cowered before it when the cherubim held swords of flame to bar them from their garden home. When Solomon completed the building of the first temple, he brought in all the things which David, his father, had dedicated for the temple and put the silver and gold and the engraved vessels among the treasures of the house of the Lord. Then he assembled the elders of Israel and all the heads of the tribes, the chiefs of the fathers of the children of Israel, that they might bring up the ark of the covenant of the Lord out of Zion, the city of David.

All the people of Israel assembled themselves before King Solomon, and all the elders came, and the priests took up the ark, and untold sheep and oxen were sacrificed. And the priests brought the ark of the covenant of the Lord into the Holy of Holies, under the wings of the cherubim. And there was nothing in the ark except the two stone tablets which Moses had put there at Horeb, the tablets of the covenant which the Lord had made with the children of Israel.

When the priests came out of the sanctuary, the cloud filled the temple of the Lord, and the priests could not bear to minister because of the cloud, for the glory of the Creator of the Galaxies had filled the house of the Lord.

When did we last see that light in the sanctuary of one of our churches, of no matter what denomination or affiliation? Perhaps it is there, but we may not recognize it because we are afraid of it. We have become so bound by the restrictions of the choices made over the past centuries that we cannot see it. We are afraid of that which we cannot control; so we continue to draw in the boundaries around us, to limit ourselves to what we can know and understand. Thus we lose our human calling because we do not dare to be creators, co-creators with God.

Artists have always been drawn to the wild, wide elements they cannot control or understand—the sea, mountains, fire. To be an artist means to approach the light, and that means to let go our control, to allow our whole selves to be placed with absolute faith in that which is greater than we are. The novel we sit down to write and the one we end up writing may be very different, just as the Jesus we grasp and the Jesus who grasps us may also differ.

We live under the illusion that if we can acquire complete control, we can understand God or we can write the great American novel. But the only way we can brush against the hem of the Lord or hope to be part of the creative process, is to have the courage, the faith, to abandon control.

For the opposite of sin is faith and never virtue, and we live in a world which believes that self-control can make us virtuous. But that's not how it

works. How many men and women we have en-
countered, of great personal virtue and moral rec-
titude, convinced of their own righteousness, who
have also been totally insensitive to the needs of
others and sometimes downright cruel! Surely
Elizabeth Barrett's father was convinced that he was
right. To quote H. A. Williams again,

> When I attempt to make myself virtuous, the me
> I can thus organize and discipline is no more
> than the me of which I am aware. And it is pre-
> cisely the equation of my total self with this one
> small part of it which is the root cause of all sin.
> This is the fundamental mistake often made in
> exhortations to repentance and amendment.
> They attempt to confirm me in my lack of faith
> by getting me to organize the self I know against
> the self I do not know.

In prayer, in the creative process, these two parts
of ourselves, the mind and the heart, the intellect
and the intuition, the conscious and the subconscious mind, stop fighting each other and collaborate. Theophan the Recluse advised those who
came to him for counsel to "pray with the mind in
the heart," and surely this is how the artist works.
When mind and heart work together, they *know*
each other as two people who love each other
know; and as the love of two people is a gift, a
totally unmerited, incomprehensible gift, so is
the union of mind and heart. David cried out to
God, "Unite my heart to fear thy name." It is my
prayer, too.

When I urge that we abandon our rigid self-control I am not suggesting that we abandon ourselves into hysteria or licentiousness, uninhibited temper tantrums or self-indulgence. Anything but. However, when we try to control our lives totally with the self we think we know, "the result is that growth in self-awareness is inhibited." And, Williams continues, "there is a sort of devilish perversity in this organizing me not to sin by means of the very thing which ensures that I shall. Faith, on the other hand, consists in the awareness that I am more than I know." Such awareness came to the prodigal when he realized that he was more than a starving swineherd. What led him home was his becoming aware that he was also his father's son. Yet his awareness of sonship was enough to make him journey homewards.

The journey homewards. Coming home. That's what it's all about. The journey to the coming of the kingdom. That's probably the chief difference between the Christian and the secular artist—the purpose of the work, be it story or music or painting, is to further the coming of the kingdom, to make us aware of our status as children of God, and to turn our feet toward home.

Berdyaev expresses it thus:

All the products of man's genius may be temporal and corruptible, but the creative fire itself is eternal, and everything temporal ought to be consumed in it. It is the tragedy of creativeness that it wants eternity and the eternal, but produces the temporal, and builds up culture which is in time and a part of history. The creative act is an escape from the power of time and ascent to the divine. . . .

Most artists are aware that during the deepest moments of that creation they are out on the other side of themselves and so are free from time, with the same joyousness that comes in the greatest moments of prayer.

"Creativeness," Berdyaev continues,

is the struggle against the consequences of sin, the expression of man's true vocation, but creativeness is distorted and debased by sin. Hence the ethics of creativeness deal with the agonizing struggle of the human spirit. Creativeness needs purification, needs the purifying fire.

Or, as T. S. Eliot puts it:

Who then devised the torment? Love.
Love is the unfamiliar Name
Behind the hands that wove
The intolerable shirt of flame
Which human power cannot remove.
  We only live, only suspire,
  Consumed by either fire or fire.

It takes great faith to open oneself to this purifying fire, to believe that it is the power of love. The extraordinary thing is that it is often imaged as a fire of roses. Eliot concludes *Little Gidding,* from which I have just quoted, with these lines:

When the tongues of flame are in-folded
Into the crowned knot of fire
And the fire and the rose are one.

In *The Princess and the Goblin,* George MacDonald describes the fire of roses into which the princess must plunge her hands to be burned and purified. And Dante uses this metaphor in *The Divine Comedy.* Where did the fire of roses originate? I suspect that it goes back beyond human memory.

Dare we open ourselves to this purifying fire, to believe that it is the power of love? H. A. Williams continues,

> Such faith cannot be contrived. If it were contrivable, if it were something I could create in myself by following some recipe or other, then it would not be faith. It would be works—my organizing the self I know. That faith can be only the gift of God emphasizes the scandal of our human condition—the scandal of our absolute dependence on him. I have to depend completely upon what very largely I do not know and cannot control.

The artist knows total dependence on the unseen reality. The paradox is that the creative process is incomplete unless the artist is, in the best and most proper sense of the word, a technician, one who knows the tools of his trade, has studied his techniques, is disciplined. One writer said, "If I leave my work for a day, it leaves me for three." I think it was Artur Rubinstein who admitted, "If I don't practice the piano for one day I know it. If I don't practice it for two days my family knows it. If I don't practice it for three days, my public knows it."

The moment of inspiration does not come to someone who lolls around expecting the gift to be free. It is no giveaway. It is the pearl for which we have to pay a great price, the price of intense loneliness, the price of that vulnerability which often allows us to be hurt; the less readily understandable price of hurting those we love, even though in less radical ways than Gauguin's. And I am not sure it's a choice. If we're given a gift—and the size of the gift, great or small, is irrelevant—then most of us must serve it, like it or not. I say most of us because I have seen people of great talent who have done nothing with it and who mutter about getting down to work "when there's time."

For a woman who has chosen family as well as work, there's never time, and yet somehow time is given to us as time is given to the man who must sail a ship or chart the stars. For most writers it takes many manuscripts before enough royalties are coming in to pay for a roof over the head and bread on the table. Other jobs must often be found to take care of bread and butter. A certain amount of stubbornness—pig-headedness—is essential.

I'm often asked how my children feel about my work, and I have to reply, "Ambivalent." Our first-born observed to me many years ago, when she was a grade-school child, "Nobody else's mother writes books." But she also said, around the same time, "Mother, you've been very cross and edgy with us lately, and we've noticed that you haven't been writing, and we wish you'd get back to the typewriter. " A wonderfully freeing remark. I had to learn that I was a better mother and wife when I was working than when I was not.

While our son was in college he was very careful that nobody knew that his father was Dr. Charles Tyler in *All My Children,* nor that his mother had written *A Wrinkle in Time.*

And once when our children ranged in age from eight to thirteen, we said to one of their teachers that we did not understand why they were so concerned about their report cards; we did not pressure them; we wanted them to enjoy learning, and this was much more important to us than grades. The teacher looked at us and said, "Don't you realize that you, yourselves, are pressure?"

We didn't. Or we hadn't, not until that moment. But if I think on it, I suppose that most parents cause a certain amount of ambivalence and pressure for their children, and ours haven't yet turned us in.

I was at the annual meeting of a state library association a few years later, when the children were in the process of leaving the nest, and one of the librarians asked me, "What do you think you and Hugh have done which was best for your children?"

I answered immediately and without thinking, "We love each other."

A life lived in chaos is an impossibility for the artist. No matter how unstructured may seem the painter's garret in Paris or the poet's pad in Greenwich Village, the artist must have some kind of order or he will produce a very small body of work. To create a *work* of art, great or small, is *work*, hard work, and work requires discipline and order.

I learned slowly that, for me, this must be external as well as internal. My last year in boarding school I almost lost my "Honor Pin" every month because I had almost accumulated those fatal ten "disorder marks." It was when I was in college and my roommate and I chose our own room and it was ours that I learned that I worked better in a tidy nest. I am not the greatest housekeeper in the world, but my house is tidy.

One problem with the word *work* is that it has come to be equated with drudgery, and is considered degrading. Now, some work *is* drudgery though it is not always degrading. Vacuuming the house or scrubbing out the refrigerator is drudgery for me, though I find it in no way degrading. And that it is drudgery is a lack in me. I enjoy the results and so I should enjoy producing the results. I suspect that it is not the work itself which is the problem but that it is taking me from other work, such as whatever manuscript I am currently working on. Drudgery is not what work is meant to be. Our work should be our play. If we watch a child at play for a few minutes, *seriously* at play, we see that all his energies are concentrated on it. He is working very hard at it. And that is how the artist works, although the artist may be conscious of discipline while the child simply experiences it.

I watched my small son trying to build a tower from blocks which had already been used by so many children that corners had been chipped off, edges worn. They were not as easy to balance as they had been when they were new.

The tower would start to rise. Then he would place a block on one which was uneven, and the whole thing would topple. With a shout of outrage he would begin again.

I watched, unnoticed, while he started the tower three, four, five times, unwilling to give up. Tears of frustration were streaming down his face. From his small lungs came uninhibited roars of fury. But he kept at it until the tower stood, a leaning Pisa kind of tower, but a tower.

Work? Play?

In this last stretch of the twentieth century we are losing the ability to equate work with play, and there are many self-evident reasons for this. One publishing house, owned by a conglomerate, was told that it must drop from its list any book which did not sell a mandatory number of copies during a year. And so the works of a poet such as Yeats have been discarded, are no longer available, are out of print.

Greed is not the only reason for this. Too many books are published which are shabbily and shoddily written. Many are simply rough drafts, and most first drafts need long and hard revision, and that means work, and we have been taught to look down on work. But one reason for this is that much work is not, in fact, work but drudgery.

Hugh and I are among the world's lucky ones, reminding ourselves frequently how fortunate we both are to be doing work which we love, work which is, for us, play.

Perhaps *play* is the answer to those who condemn what they call the "Puritan work ethic," which provides us a mental image of drably clad, dour-faced people grimly doing their duty. This has little to do with either those imprisoned in the drudgery of sweatshops or those of us who have been given the joy of work we love, be it work with children, words, paint, the discoveries of vaccines, chipping beauty out of marble, weaving melody out of seemingly random notes.

Many people in walks of life which do not involve creation are completely unaware of the necessity for discipline. It is not only that few serious artists who live lives of debauchery produce a large body of work but that few serious artists are able to live lives which are without interruption. We do not shed all obligations when the children leave home. I am working on this section of this manuscript while teaching an intensive four-and-a-half hour credit course, and neither may be skimped. Many writers work in the evenings after a nine-to-five job. And there are letters to be answered, the phone which constantly calls us. I travel a lot in order to give lectures, teach at writer's conferences (though most of my destinations are not as glamourous as Cyprus). To write consistently, I must seize opportunities. I write in airports. I write on planes. I find airports and planes and hotel rooms excellent places in which to write because while I am in them I am not responsible for anything except my work. Once I have my seat assignment I can write until the flight is called; when I am on the plane, the pilot is responsible for the flight, I am not, and so I can work on my manuscript. In a hotel room I do not have to think about the vacuum cleaner (though sometimes I would like to have one); domestic chores are not my responsibility; I am free to write.

No matter where I am, at home, abroad, I begin the day with morning prayer, including the psalms for the day, so that at the end of each month I have gone through the book of Psalms. I also read from both the Old and New Testaments. And there is almost always something in the Psalms or the other Scripture which I need to hear for that day, something I may have read hundreds of times before, but which suddenly springs out at me with new meaning.

I end the day in the same way, with evening prayer, and this gives the day a structure. Between these two joyful disciplines, the day is also moderately structured. I write all morning. Lunch is often shared with a friend. Then, most afternoons, I return to my manuscript, though if I've put in a hard and productive morning's work I don't feel bound by this. I may need to go to the library for research. When we are at Crosswicks I usually take time to go to the brook, taking heavy clippers with me to try to keep the bittersweet from strangling the trees, to cut new paths to the rocks overlooking the water or leading to a particularly beautiful grove of birch or pine. Sitting or, better, lying on one of my favorite sun-warmed rocks, I try to take time to let go, to listen, in much the same way that I listen when I am writing. This is praying time, and the act of listening in prayer is the same act as listening in writing. And again, comparisons need not come into it; the prayer of the saint is not necessarily "better" than the prayer of the peasant.

And then there is time in which to be, simply to be, that time in which God quietly tells us who we are and who he wants us to be. It is then that God can take our emptiness and fill it up with what he wants and drain away the business with which we inevitably get involved in the dailiness of human living.

CHAPTER ELEVEN

THE OTHER SIDE OF SILENCE

t is a joy to be allowed to be the servant of the work. And it is a humbling and exciting thing to know that my work knows more than I do. Throughout the years there have been many proofs of this, but I think I began to understand it more fully as I worked on *A Wrinkle in Time,* my seventh book to be published, eleventh to be written. As I tried to serve it I began to comprehend something about listening to the work, about going where it shoved me. And so the long two years of rejection slips which followed were especially difficult; it wasn't just that my work was being rejected, or, if it was, it meant that I had not even begun to serve the work.

While I was writing I'd given myself a crash course in physics, having managed in my schooling to avoid as much as possible anything even remotely mathematical. I didn't get interested because I was working on a story based on the theories of contemporary, post-Newtonian physics but because post-Newtonian physics caused me to write a story. About a year before I started work on *Wrinkle*, I discovered that higher math is easier to understand than lower math, and in reading the works of the great mathematicians and physicists I was discovering theological insights I had not found in my determined efforts to read theology. The discovery of physics preceded the work on the book.

So it has been a surprise and a delight to me to discover that my friends who are scientists, my son-in-law, Peter, who is a theoretical chemist, my godson, John, who is an immunologist, find the science in my fantasies to be "real" and have passed them around to their friends. This is marvellous proof that my books know more than I know.

The fact that *Wrinkle* is deeply embedded in both theology and physics had little to do with me, and this puts me in my proper place as a servant struggling (never completely succeeding) to be faithful to the work, the work which slowly and gently tries to teach me some of what it knows. Sometimes it is years after a book is published that I discover what some of it meant. For instance, when I made the villain in *Wrinkle* a disembodied brain, It, that was just how the villain happened to look; I wasn't consciously realizing that the brain, when it is disengaged from the heart, turns vicious. (Conversely, the heart, when it is disengaged from the brain, can become sentimental and untruthful.)

It is nothing short of miraculous that I am so often given, during the composition of a story, just what I need at the very moment that I need it. *Why* did I blunder into the discovery of physics just as I was ready to write *Wrinkle*? *Why* did the names Mrs Whatsit, Mrs Who, and Mrs Which come as we were driving along in the station wagon with our children?

When I was roughing out *A Wind in the Door,* trying to listen, I knew that something wasn't working. I had the characters, Meg and Charles Wallace and Calvin and their families; I had the cherubim, Progo; the three Mr. Jenkinses; and the snake, Louise the Larger. But the story was not unfolding. I couldn't hear where it wanted me to go. And at that moment my physician friend, Pat, to whom the book is dedicated, gave me two articles from the *New England Medical Journal,* by Lewis Thomas, on mitochondria, those strange microcosmic creatures living their own lives within our cells, using us as their host planet but living independently of us, with their own DNA and RNA. And there was where the story wanted me to go, away from the macrocosm and into the microcosm. What made Pat, at that specific time, give me exactly what I needed—or what the book needed? Of course it didn't come free; it never does. With the help of my elder daughter I gave myself a crash course in cellular biology, which science didn't even exist when I was in school—and if it had existed, I'd probably have avoided it. Hard work, that crash course, but lots of fun.

When I was well into *A Swiftly Tilting Planet* I had set myself all kinds of problems which I feared might be insoluble. I was trying to listen to the story and was thoroughly confused because in the story I'd been given a vengeful South American dictator in a small country called Vespugia (my husband thought up that delightful name) set in the middle of what used to be known as Patagonia, a sizeable area along what are now the boundaries of Chile and Argentina. I also had in the story an ancient Welsh prince, Madoc, son of Owain, King of Gwynedd, who, after his father's death and the violent quarreling of the brothers over the throne, had left Wales and was supposed to have come to North America, before Leif Erickson, and to have made his life among a tribe of friendly Indians. The legend persists today, and Madoc and his descendants were important to the story, and so was the Vespugian dictator, Mad Dog Branzillo. And what I needed was some kind of a link between Wales and South America, particularly, of course, the Vespugian part of South America, and it seemed to me extremely unlikely that there could be such a connection. I was afraid I had painted myself into a corner.

And just at that time off I went to Wheaton College to give some lectures. I remember standing in the library and saying that I needed to know more about the legend of Madoc. I didn't mention Vespugia or Patagonia or my need for a link. Ruth Cording loaned me two little paperback volumes, Welsh on one side of the page, English on the other, about Wales and America, and in one of these books I read that in 1865 an expedition left Wales to go to settle in South America, in exactly that part of Patagonia where I had placed Vespugia.

How to explain this? I can't. But it strikes me as more than that I was unknowingly dipping into the collective unconscious. My guardian angel was certainly working overtime, and I accepted the miracle with awe and gratitude, and I owe yet another debt to Wheaton, and to Mrs. Cording, who has since managed to find for me my very own copies of these two books which were so important for the background of *A Swiftly Tilting Planet.*

When I first started sending *Wrinkle* around I called it *Mrs Whatsit, Mrs Who, and Mrs Which* because that was how the book had first come to me, those three names suddenly appearing out of the blue. When Farrar, Straus, & Giroux finally decided to risk publishing it, they felt that this title sounded too juvenile, so they came up with *The Worlds of Charles Wallace.* I didn't like this but couldn't invent anything better.

This was all happening at a time when my mother was visiting us, and one morning I took her an early morning cup of coffee, and she said, "I didn't sleep well last night, but I think I've got a title for you, right out of the text: *A Wrinkle in Time.*"

"You've got it, Mother! That's it!"

It was. When I called the publishers they, too, were delighted. Not only titles, but sometimes some of the content of a book is from someone else, a gift which only needs to be recognized. This is in no sense plagiarism; I didn't need Lewis Thomas's words or chapters for *A Wind in the Door;* all I needed was to get excited about mitochondria. In a sense, nothing the artist produces is his in any exclusive way. An inventor takes inventory of that which is already there. A discoverer un-covers that which is. T. S. Eliot says: "Poetry takes something that we know already and turns it into something new." Perhaps art is seeing the obvious in such a new light that the old becomes new.

It isn't only in fiction that I am given these amazing gifts. When I was drawing to the close of *The Summer of the Great Grandmother,* a book about my ninety-year-old mother's last summer and her death (in her grandson's arms), my little granddaughters gave me just what I needed for the end of the book. I quote the final pages:

> The children grow in all ways. Their vocabulary advances in leaps and bounds. I am no longer Madden or Gan-mad-den. When they are formal with me, I am Grandmadeleine. Mostly it is Gran. . . .
> One night I put them to bed, and after all the songs and stories they beg for two last songs. *"Long* ones."
> So I start the *Ballad of Barbara Allen.* I have sung only a couple of verses when Charlotte says, her voice quivering slightly, "Gran, you *know* that's a bad one."
> "What, Charlotte?"
> "You *know* that's a bad one."
> Both Barbara Allen and her young man are dead and buried at the end of the ballad; I ask, "Why, Charlotte? Because it's sad?"
> "No! Because she didn't love *anybody."*

Charlotte knows what it is all about. The refusal to love is the only unbearable thing.

Another time, when Josephine and Alan (the parents) are away, I tell the rest of the family that I'll put the little girls to bed and go to bed early myself and finish reading a manuscript. We've had a very happy evening; the little girls—no longer babies—and I had a long bath hour before dinner; we had a lovely meal, with the menu chosen by the children: chicken salad and peas. I added potato salad and a big green salad. It's warm this evening, so the mostly cold meal was just right.

After dinner the children and I sing songs and tell stories while I get them into their nightgowns, and all is comfortable and familiar and safe and loving. We go into the bathroom to brush teeth and wash faces, and suddenly Léna looks at me and asks, "Grandmadeleine, is it all right?"

Slightly taken aback . . . I answer, "Yes, Léna, it's all right."

"But, Gran, is everything really all right? really?" It is completely cosmic questioning, coming from a small girl in a white nightgown with a toothbrush in her hand, sensing the unfamiliar surrounding the familiar. It is warm and light in the house, but the greater the radius of light, the wider the perimeter of darkness.

"Yes, Léna," I answer again. I think of Greatie fleeing a burning house as shots spattered the water about the little boat, and years later being rowed down that same river to visit the African princess. I think of Mado, holding a dying Yankee

boy in her arms, her love and compassion concentrated wholly on his need, despite her own
bereavement. I think of my mother watching her
husband cough his lungs out in the cold light of
the Alps and of my father setting his name down
on the empty page of the diary for the new year.
It was not a tranquil world for my grandchildren's forebears, and it is in the lives of these
long-gone men and women that I find the answer
to Léna's question. I must answer it for her, looking down at her serious, upturned face, and I
can answer truthfully only if I have my feet
planted very firmly on rock.

I think of the warmth of the rock at the brook
and that I will never know more than a glimpse
of the *ousia* of the small green frog—or of my
mother—or of the two little girls—

and this is all right, too.

"Is it *really* all right?" Léna persists.

"Yes, Léna, it is all right."

And the two little girls and I climb into the
four-poster bed to sing songs and tell stories.

What made those two little girls insist on the affirmation of love and all-rightness just as I was ending my book?

Perhaps the only part I had in it was accepting
the discipline of listening or training the ability to
recognize something when it is offered.

Sometimes the gift is offered so magnanimously
that no training is needed. While I was working on
A Ring of Endless Light and having the fun of in-

troducing Vicky Austin (of *Meet the Austins, The Moon by Night, The Young Unicorns*) to Adam Eddington (of *The Arm of the Starfish*), it became apparent to me that Vicky was going to have to describe how a dolphin feels, and I knew that I couldn't write the description until I, myself, had felt a dolphin. There are not many dolphins around the island of Manhattan nor the hills around Crosswicks. Just as I had come to the point where I could no longer put off the scene where Vicky meets a dolphin, I flew out to San Diego to teach at a writer's conference. And I spent happy hours at Sea World, petting dolphins, at first tentatively patting their heads, then stroking their beautiful bodies, then discovering that they love to have their chests scratched—just what I needed, given me in a great unexpected gift at exactly the moment I needed it.

I don't pretend to understand any of this in the language of provable fact, but that is the language of works, the language of man's control, not the language of faith.

I only know that the gifts are given and that I believe in them.

H. A. Williams continues, "Justification by faith means that I have nothing else on which to depend except my receptivity to what I can never own or manage. And this very capacity to receive cannot be the result of effort. Faith is something given, not achieved. It is created by God's word in Christ."

For the Christian writer, that's what the creative process is all about.

Can one be a Christian artist and not know it?

I think that's the way it always happens, even when one is constantly struggling to be Christian in daily living. I cannot try, consciously, to write a "Christian" story—even in such a book as *Dance in the Desert* which (although it is never overtly stated) is about the holy family's flight into Egypt. When I am working, I move into an area of faith which is beyond the conscious control of my intellect. I do not mean that I discard my intellect, that I am an anti-intellectual, gung-ho for intuition and intuition only. Like it or not, I *am* an intellectual. The challenge is to let my intellect work *for* the creative act, not against it. And this means, first of all, that I must have more faith in the work than I have in myself.

When I start working on a book, which is usually several years and several books before I start to *write* it, I am somewhat like a French peasant cook. There are several pots on the back of the stove, and as I go by during the day's work, I drop a carrot in one, an onion in another, a chunk of meat in another. When it comes time to prepare the meal, I take the pot which is most nearly full and bring it to the front of the stove.

So it is with writing. There are several pots on those back burners. An idea for a scene goes into one, a character into another, a description of a tree in the fog into another. When it comes time to write, I bring forward the pot which has the most in it. The dropping in of ideas is sometimes quite conscious; sometimes it happens without my realizing it. I look, and something has been added which is just what I need, but I don't remember when it was added.

When it is time to start work, I look at everything in the pot, sort, arrange, think about character and story line. Most of this part of the work is done consciously, but then there comes a moment of unselfconsciousness, of letting go and serving the work.

That statement of H. A. Williams continues to stimulate me: "The me I can thus organize and discipline is no more than the me of which I am aware. And it is precisely the equation of my total self with this one small part of it which is the root cause of all sin."

Sin, that unpopular word again. The worse things get, the more we try to rationalize and alibi. When we do wrong we try to fool ourselves (and others) that it is because our actions and reactions have been coded into our genetic pattern at the moment of conception. Or our mothers didn't understand us. Or they understood us too well. Or it is the fault of society. Certainly it is never our fault, and therefore we have not sinned.

And by such dirty devices any shred of free will left in the human being is taken away. If I do wrong I may do it unwittingly, thinking I am doing something for the best; but if it turns out to be wrong, I have done it, and I must bear the responsibility.

It is not somebody else's or something else's fault. If it is I am less than human.

Like everybody else, I tend to rationalize and alibi before I let myself admit, "Yes, I did this. I am sorry. I will do whatever I can to make reparation." Our sins defeat us unless we are willing to recognize them, confess them, and so become healed and whole and holy—not qualified, mind you, just holy.

I first met Harry Williams while he was still at Cambridge and before he had become an Anglican monk at the Community of the Resurrection in Yorkshire. His Christianity shone from him. I had already read much of his work up until then, and I sat at his feet and learned—about myself and love and the Lord. It was a joy to me, a surging up-rush of gratitude, when he, in turn, responded to some of my work. And I still learn from him, in each new book he writes.

I have a hunch that the equation of the total self with that part of the self which can be organized and disciplined is behind all "non-Christian" art (I still don't like that phrase). It is a frightening thing for many people to let go, to have faith in that which they cannot completely know and control.

But how do we *know?*

We've lost much of the richness of that word. Nowadays, *to know* means to know with the intellect. But it is a much deeper word than that. Adam *knew* Eve. To know deeply is far more than to know consciously. In the realm of faith I *know* far more than I can believe with my finite mind. I *know* that a loving God will not abandon what he creates. I *know* that the human calling is cocreation with this power of love. I *know* that neither death nor life nor angels nor principalities nor powers nor things present nor things to come nor height nor depth nor any other creature shall be able to separate us from the love of God, which is in Jesus Christ our Lord.

But in this limited world we tend to lose this kind of knowing, and this loss has permeated our fiction as well as our prayer. I've been privileged several times to speak at the University of Hawaii and have gained much richness from these experiences. In my commonplace book I've copied down the words of a Hawaiian Christian, Mother Alice Kaholusuna:

Before the missionaries came, my people used to sit outside their temples for a long time meditating and preparing themselves before entering. Then they would virtually creep to the altar to offer their petition and afterwards would again sit a long time outside, this time to "breathe life" into their prayers. The Christians, when they came, just got up, uttered a few sentences, said Amen, and were done. For that reason my people called them haoles, "without breath," or those who failed to breathe life into their prayers.

It is certainly a great witness to the power of the living Lord that Alice Kaholusuna became a Christian despite the *baoles*—as non-native Hawaiians are still called.

Her description of prayer is a beautiful description of the creative process. Meditation, silence, faith in that which we cannot control or manipulate. And letting go of that dictator self which constantly tries to take over the controls. And listening.

How far listening takes us! I'm often asked about my great scientific background, and I have no scientific background whatsoever. And the discovery of science has been an unexpected door opened for me where hitherto I had seen no break in the wall.

When I was working on *The Arm of the Starfish*, I began with my own experience. I had gone to Portugal to do research for what was later to be the novel *Love Letters*. (I don't like that title; I wanted to call it *Love Letters of a Portuguese Nun.*) Like Adam, the protagonist of *Starfish*, my husband and I took off on a Swissair jet to Lisbon; the description of the beauty of the flight is precisely as we saw it. In the morning, just as we expected to begin the descent to Lisbon, the loudspeaker came on and, just as in *Starfish*, the pilot announced that because of deep fog in Lisbon we were proceeding to Madrid. Looking out the windows of the jet we saw what Adam saw. The airport in Madrid was cold and wet and sinister. We did not have our passports questioned as Adam did, but we took the same bus into Madrid, stayed in the same hotel which looked out into the twentieth-century in front, into the Middle Ages in the rear. Like Adam we went to the Prado, saw that incredible El Greco painting of St. Francis and St. Andrew, ate the same food in the same cafeteria, were ultimately herded by bus to the airport, were fed the same meal, finally boarded the same Caravelle to Lisbon. And then the story began to take over, and Adam became involved in a kidnapping and a plot of international intrigue. It was an exciting plot, and I thought I had the story pretty well under control. I had long and carefully worked out what was going to happen to Adam and the other characters.

Then something unexpected happened. Adam had gone nearly three nights without sleep and was finally allowed to go to bed in Lisbon, in the Ritz hotel (where we spent two luxurious nights). He plunged into that deep and restful sleep which comes to the healthy body. Finally, slept out, he woke up, and there, sitting in a chair and looking at him, was a young man called Joshua. Adam was very surprised to see Joshua. Madeleine was even more surprised to see Joshua. There had been no Joshua in my plot at all.

I had a choice at that moment. I could ignore Joshua, refuse to allow him into my story. Or I could have faith in the creative process and listen to Joshua. This meant a great deal of rewriting—probably 150 or more pages. I cannot now imagine the book without Joshua, and I know that it is a much better book because of him. But where he came from I cannot say. He was a sheer gift of grace.

It has been pointed out to me that Joshua is a Christ figure, and of course the name *Joshua* is a form of *Jesus*. But if I had consciously thought, *I will put a Christ figure into this book*, I could not possibly have done it. I knew, deep in my heart, that when Joshua arrived, so named, he was probably going to have to give his life, and so it turned out.

And here is another interesting part of the creative process: I knew that if I *felt* anything while I was writing about Joshua's death, the scene would end up in the wastepaper basket. Emotion can come before writing and after writing, but it must not be present during writing.

In one of his letters, Tchekov writes, "You may weep and moan over your stories, you may suffer together with your heroes, but I consider one must do this so that the reader does not notice it. The more objective, the stronger will be the effect."

I also find helpful an analogy from my husband's discipline, the theatre. Nothing is easier than to have hysterics on the stage, to rant and rail and weep. Back during my own days in the theatre, one of my favourite roles was that of a vindictive Victorian wife, who ultimately has hysterics at the top of a flight of stairs and falls, screaming, all the way to the bottom. Very flashy but probably not very moving.

If the actor or actress is caught up in emotion during a performance, the audience may admire the acting but seldom feels the emotion because that contrasting background is not there. The place for emotion in the actor is during rehearsal, where he must go through everything his character goes through, feel everything his character feels, weep, laugh, *be* the character. But in performance the actor must be in charge of his medium; and by that I mean not that he controls the performance, leaving no openings for surprise, but that his technique is perfected.

When you tell a funny story, if you laugh while you're telling it, the audience won't. The more effective technique is deadpan. It's a strange paradox:

your technique must be practiced until it is as close to perfect as you can make it, and then, and then only, are you free to let go, to let yourself get out of the way.

When I finally came to the day when I had to write the scene of Joshua's death, I approached it, I think, somewhat in the way that Mother Alice Kaholusuna describes approaching the temple. I began to write, and by some grace I was got out of the way. I was, somehow, out on the other side of myself. When I had finished the scene I came back to myself, exhausted, sorrowful, and simultaneously strangely joyful.

When I am writing, on the other side of silence, as it were, and I am interrupted, there is an incredible shock as I am shoved through the sound barrier, the light barrier, out of the real world and into what seems, at least for the first few moments, a less real world.

The same thing is true in prayer, in meditation. For the disciplines of the creative process and Christian contemplation are almost identical.

I was working on the final chapters of *Starfish* during the summer, in Crosswicks, and quite often while my mother rested after lunch I would read to her what I had written during the morning. If our ten-year-old son was around, he was likely to sit on the edge of the bed and listen, and he was there the afternoon that I read of Joshua's death.

He got very excited and upset. "Change it," he demanded.

"I can't. That's what happened."

"But you're the writer. You can change it."

"I can't. I didn't want Joshua to get shot either, but that's what happened. I couldn't stop it."

"But you *can*. You're the writer!"

But I couldn't. And at that point in his development, I couldn't make him understand that I couldn't. He was so angry with me for allowing Joshua to die that he wouldn't read anything else I wrote for several years.

Now he has grown up and understands that the artist cannot change the work at whim but can only listen, look, wait, and set down what is revealed.

All that extra work when Joshua appeared in Adam's hotel room was no small thing. But neither was it unusual, and I wrote two or three times the 150 pages before finishing the book. As with all my books, *Starfish* was more rewritten than written, and with each subsequent book the need to rewrite becomes more rather than less. As the writer struggles to grow in knowledge of techniques, characterization, theme, more and more work becomes necessary. My beloved English nanny, Mrs. O, was fond of remarking, "Hard work's not easy." Of the lazy, she said, "He loves work so much he could lie down beside it."

If I need a reminder that hard work's not easy, all I have to do is look at Crosswicks. It's a plain New England farmhouse, built approximately 225 years ago, when there were no bulldozers, power saws, backhoes, or any of the machinery we take for granted. Everything had to be made by hand, applied by hand. The single majestic roof-tree is an awesome testimony to corporate strength; surely everyone worked together to build this comfortable home. And they were full of faith: the doors are cross-and-Bible doors; the hardware is H-, Help, Lord. Simple though the house is, it is a work of art and a witness to the fact that the people who built it were not afraid of work but saw work as a way of glorifying God.

The writer, too, should see work in this way and understand that the building of a novel is also corporate work. The writer at the desk is indeed writing in isolation, but (for me, at least) this isolation must be surrounded by community, be it the community of family, village, church, city.

Joshua came to me as a free gift, but the paradox has always been that such a gift is dearly bought.

The joyful acceptance that readers create my books along with me and share their creation in their letters, helps me to grow, to be more daring than I would be able to be otherwise. In trying to share what I believe, I am helped to discover what I do, in fact, believe, which is often more than I realize. I am given hope that I will remember how to walk across the water.

I'm still not a great deal more certain what a Christian artist is than when I was first approached to talk about the subject. I am, perhaps, a little more articulate but not much more certain.

A Christian artist sees work as being for the glory of God. Yes.

And a Christian artist cares what the children see. Yes, but I'd let them see lots more than is considered proper. I'd give them the whole Bible, uncut, taking out none of the sex, none of the violence, knowing that the Bible balances itself and that they will do their own automatic deleting.

It strikes me as odd indeed that in this day when the churches, by and large, think they are so freed up about sex, the Episcopal Church still leaves the Song of Songs out of the daily lectionary. I would not take from the children the exuberance of this sheerly erotic love poetry because it will have nothing to say to them till they are at the age of falling in love. And gradually it will say more. To the ancient Hebrew it transcended the sexual love of male and female and spoke of God's love for his people. To the Christian it is a paean of joy about Christ's love for his Bride, the church. But it will never become transcendent for us unless we are first of all allowed to take it at its literal level.

I would not hide the human body from the children, as though it were something to be ashamed of—though neither would I flaunt it. Let it be natural and holy. The Incarnation was a total affirmation of the dignity of this body, and Paul goes on to emphasize that we are, moreover, the temple of the Holy Spirit, and if we abuse or reject or ignore our bodies, we are abusing and rejecting and ignoring this temple.

I was both amused and appalled in a rotunda in the Prado, filled with Greek and Roman statues, to see that all the genitals had been removed and covered with some kind of leaf. This prudery is in itself a form of pornography.

The balance is, as always, delicate. We seldom find the center. We are constantly falling off one side or the other. But the center is always there, waiting for us to discover it.

I would allow the children to ask any kind of cosmic or practical question they want to; but I would answer only the question they ask, not precede them with responses to further questions, as adults are so often tempted to do. I would share with them all of life, not hide death from them, thereby making it more fearful. Nor would I hide love, human as well as heavenly. I was amazed when the five teenaged girls in my cabin at a Congregational youth conference all told me that they were disturbed that they had never seen their parents touch each other, not to kiss, not even to hold hands. And this wasn't that long ago.

Perhaps it is never, in the long run, I who will make the decision as to what to let the children see. If I listen, I will know. It is another of those things which does not belong in the realm of do-it-yourself.

But it does make a difference. It is part of my becoming Christian—for it is never a *fait accompli*; it is always a becoming.

CHAPTER TWELVE

FEEDING THE LAKE

Vulnerability is something we instinctively reject because we are taught from kindergarten on that we must protect ourselves, control our behaviour and our lives. But in becoming man for us, Christ made himself totally vulnerable for us in Jesus of Nazareth, and it is not possible to be a Christian while refusing to be vulnerable.

I am beginning to see that almost every definition I find of being a Christian is also a definition of being an artist.

And a Christian artist?

We care about what the children see.

We are, ourselves, as little children, and therefore we are vulnerable. We might paraphrase Descartes to read, "I hurt; therefore I am."

And because of the great affirmation of the Incarnation, we may not give in to despair.

Nor superstition.

Being a Christian, being saved, does not mean that nothing bad is ever going to happen. Terrible things happen to Christians as well as to Hindus and Buddhists and hedonists and atheists. To human beings. When the phone rings at an unexpected hour my heart lurches. I love; therefore I am vulnerable.

When we were children, we used to think that when we were grown up we would no longer be vulnerable. But to grow up is to accept vulnerability.

During the question-and-answer period after a talk, a college student rose in the audience and commented with some surprise, "You don't seem to feel any conflict between science and religion!"

I tried to explain. Of course not. Why should there be a conflict? All that the new discoveries of science can do is to enlarge our knowledge of the magnitude and glory of God's creation. We may, and often do, abuse our discoveries, use them for selfish and greedy purposes, but it is the abuse which causes the conflict, not the discoveries themselves. When they upset the religious establishment it is not because they have done anything to diminish God; they only diminish, or—even more frightening—change, the current establishment's definition of God. We human beings tend to reject change, but a careful reading of Scripture reveals the slow and unwilling acceptance of change in the ancient Hebrews' understanding of the Master of the Universe, and the Incarnation demanded more change than the establishment could bear. But our fear and our rejection does not take away from truth, and truth is what the Bible instructs us to know in order that we may be free.

Neither our knowledge of God and his purposes for his creation nor the discoveries of science are static. I must admit that the scientists are often easier for me to understand than the theologians, for many theologians say, "These are the final answers." Whereas the scientists—correction: the best of them—say, "This is how it appears now. If further evidence is to the contrary, we will see where it leads us."

And of course I'm being unfair to the theologians. The best of them, too, are open to this uncertainty, which is closer to the truth that will set us free than any closed system.

One of the impulses behind all creativity is a divine discontent with the shadows on the wall of the cave, which appear to be the truth but which do not expand us creatively. We have many mythic ways of expressing this. One is the superb story of Adam and Eve, tempted by pride "to be as God," and later turned out of Eden. We human beings were meant to be something which we are not.

Homo sapiens. "Man who knows." Or rather, "man who is conscious" would be more accurate. Man who is conscious that he does not know. Has there been a loss of knowing since Adam and Eve, rather than a gain? Despite all our technology there is far more that we do not know than that we know, and the most terrible defect is our inability to tell right from wrong, to do horrible things for all the right reasons, and then to blunder inadvertently into doing something which turns out to be good. We try to make the loving, the creative, decision, but we cannot *know* whether or not we are right.

Alleluia! We don't have to be right! We do have to love, to be vulnerable, to accept joy and pain, and to grow through them.

Was it predetermined that Milton go blind in order to write *Paradise Lost*? That Beethoven go deaf to write the Ninth Symphony? That these artists grew through affliction is undeniable, but that this affliction was planned? No! Everything in me rebels. I cannot live in a world where everything is predetermined, an ant world in which there is no element of choice. I do believe that we all have a share in the writing of our own story. We do make a decision at the crossroads. Milton could have retreated into passive blindness and self-pity instead of trying the patience of his three dutiful daughters and any visiting friend by insisting that they write down what he dictated. Beethoven could have remained in the gloom of silence instead of forging the glorious sounds which he could never hear except in his artist's imagination. Sometimes the very impetus of overcoming obstacles results in a surge of creativity. It is in our responses that we are given the gift of helping God write our story.

During the Second World War one of my friends

was an Englishwoman who was married to an R.A.F. officer. Daily she walked with vulnerability, not knowing whether or not his plane would be shot down. One day he was allowed an unexpected leave before a dangerous mission and came home to London for a brief visit with his wife and three small children. Joyfully, she left him at home, took all their food coupons, and went shopping to prepare as festive a meal as could be procured in wartime London. While she was gone there was an unexpected daytime raid, and her house was hit. Her husband, her three children, were killed.

During the rest of the war she worked hard, was helpful to many other people, did her passionate grieving in private. Ultimately she met a man who fell in love with her and asked her to marry him. It was, she said, the most difficult decision she had ever had to make in her life. If she did not marry again, if she had no more children, she was safe; she could not be hurt again as she had been hurt. If she remarried, if she had more babies, she was opening herself to total vulnerability. It is easier to be safe than to be vulnerable.

But she made the dangerous decision. She dared to love again.

I told this story once at a college, and during a reception a handsome young philosophy professor came up to me; she had been married, and her husband had died; she told me that she was not going to do as the Englishwoman had done; she was never going to open herself to that kind of pain again; she refused to be vulnerable.

I do not think that I would want to be a student in her philosophy classes.

To be alive is to be vulnerable. To be born is to start the journey towards death. If taxes have not always been inevitable, death has. What, then, does life mean? No more than "Out, brief candle"?

The artist struggles towards meaning. Mahler was terrified of death and worked out his fear in music. I had a letter from a college student at Harvard saying, "I am afraid of nonbeing." That same day, a friend with whom I was having lunch said, "I cannot bear the thought of annihilation."

Art is an affirmation of life, a rebuttal of death.

And here we blunder into paradox again, for during the creation of any form of art, art which affirms the value and the holiness of life, the artist must die.

To serve a work of art, great or small, is to die, to die to self. If the artist is to be able to listen to the work, he must get out of the way; or, more correctly, since getting out of the way is not a do-it-yourself activity, he must be willing to be got out of the way, to be killed to self (as Juan Carlos Ortiz sees the mythic killing of baptism) in order to become the servant of the work.

To serve a work of art is almost identical with adoring the Master of the Universe in contemplative prayer. In contemplative prayer the saint (who knows himself to be a sinner, for none of us is whole, healed, and holy twenty-four hours a day) turns inwards in what is called "the prayer of the heart," not to find self, but to lose self in order to be found.

We have been afraid of this kind of prayer, we of

the twentieth-century Judeo-Christian tradition. It is not talked about in many temples or churches. And so those intuitively seeking it have been forced to look for it elsewhere.

Why have we been afraid of it? Because it is death, and no matter how loudly we protest, we are afraid of death.

Many young people have asked me about Hindu or Buddhist or Sufi methods of meditation and are astounded, and sometimes disbelieving, when I tell them that we have such a Way within our own tradition.

The techniques of contemplation are similar in all traditions, just as the pianist, no matter what kind of music he is going to play, must do his finger exercises. But ultimately the aim is different. For the Easterner the goal is *nirvana,* which means "where there is no wind," and for us the wind of the Spirit is vital, even when it blows harshly. We do not move from meditation into contemplation, into self-annihilation, into death, in order to be freed from the intolerable wheel of life. No. We move—are moved—into death in order to be discovered, to be loved into truer life by our Maker. To die to self in the prayer of contemplation is to move to a meeting of lovers.

The great artists, dying to self in their work, collaborate with their work, know it and are known by it as Adam knew Eve, and so share in the mighty act of Creation.

That is our calling, the calling of all of us, but perhaps it is simplest for the artist (at work, at prayer) to understand, for nothing is created without this terrible entering into death. It takes great faith, faith in the work if not conscious faith in God, for dying is fearful. But without this death, nothing is born. And if we die willingly, no matter how frightened we may be, we will be found and born anew into life, and life more abundant.

Dare we all die? Willingly or unwillingly, we must, and the great artists go furthest into this unknown country.

Great art. Great artists. What about all the rest of us little people, struggling with our typewriters and tubes of paint?

The great ones are still the best mirrors for us all because the degree of the gift isn't what it's all about. It's like the presents under the Christmas tree: the ones which came from Woolworth's may be just as rejoiced over as the more expensive ones, and best of all are those which are handmade and which may have cost love rather than money. Perhaps it's something like the parable of the workers in the vineyard; maybe those who worked through the heat of the day were the Michelangelos and Leonardos and Beethovens and Tolstoys. Those who were able to work only one hour served their gift of work as best they could. And as in *Alice in Wonderland,* everybody gets prizes; there is the same quality of joy in turning a perfect bowl on the potter's wheel as in painting the Sistine Chapel.

The important thing is to recognize that our gift, no matter what the size, is indeed something given us, for which we can take no credit, but which we may humbly serve, and, in serving, learn more wholeness, be offered wondrous newness.

Picasso says that an artist paints not to ask a question but because he has found something and he wants to share—he cannot help it—what he has found.

We all feed the lake. That is what is important. It is a corporate act. During my time in the theatre I knew what it was to be part of such an enlarging of the human potential, and though I was never more than a bit player or an understudy, I knew the truth of Stanislavsky's words: "There are no small rôles. There are only small players." And I had the joy of being an instrument in the great orchestra of a play, learning from the play (how much Chekov taught me during the run of *The Cherry Orchard*), from the older actors and actresses. I was part of the Body. That's what it's all about.

When Jesus called Peter to come to him across the water, Peter, for one brief, glorious moment, remembered how and strode with ease across the lake. This is how we are meant to be, and then we forget, and we sink. But if we cry out for help (as Peter did) we will be pulled out of the water; we won't drown. And if we listen, we will hear; and if we look, we will see.

The impossible still happens to us, often during the work, sometimes when we are so tired that inadvertently we let down all the barriers we have built up. We lose our adult scepticism and become once again children who can walk down their grandmother's winding stairs without touching.

Last spring I was giving a series of talks at the Cathedral of St. Peter, in St. Petersburg, Florida, and was staying with parishioners who had a house right by the water. I was unusually tired; into an already overcrowded schedule I'd had to interject trips to England and to Jerusalem, and in Jerusalem I'd fallen and bashed in my ribs ("You've *wrinkled* your ribs," the doctor reading the X-rays told me), and I was strapped up and in considerable pain. One afternoon I had a couple of hours to myself, and so I limped to the sea wall and stretched out and closed my eyes and tried to let go all my aches and pains and tiredness, to let go and simply *be.* And while I was lying there, eased by the cool breezes, the warm sun, bursts of bird song, I heard feet coming to me across the water. It was a sound I recognized, a familiar sound: the feet of Jesus coming towards me.

And then another noise broke in, and I was back in an aching body. But I had heard. For a moment in that hearing I was freed from the dirty devices of this world. I was more than I am. I was healed.

It is one of those impossibilities I believe in; and in believing, my own feet touch the surface of the lake, and I go to meet him, like Peter, walking on water.

But only if I die first, only if I am willing to die. I

am mortal, flawed, trapped in my own skin, my own barely used brain, I do not understand this death, but I am learning to trust it. Only through this death can come the glory of resurrection; only through this death can come birth.

And I cannot do it myself. It is not easy to think of any kind of death as a gift, but it is prefigured for us in the mighty acts of Creation and Incarnation; in Crucifixion and Resurrection.

You are my helper and redeemer; make no long tarrying, O my God.

Crosswicks
June, 1980

Other Books in the WHEATON LITERARY SERIES:

Sold into Egypt: Joseph's Journey into Human Being, by Madeleine L'Engle. Cloth, 240 pages.

A Stone for a Pillow: Journeys with Jacob, by Madeleine L'Engle. Cloth, 240 pages.

The Swiftly Tilting Worlds of Madeleine L'Engle: Essays in Her Honor, by Katherine Paterson, Walter Wangerin, Jr., Eugene H. Peterson, and Others. Paper, 220 pages.

T. S. Eliot: The Philosopher Poet, by Alzina Stone Dale. Cloth, 209 pages.

The Weather of the Heart, poems by Madeleine L'Engle. Paper, 96 pages.

WinterSong: Christmas Readings, by Madeleine L'Engle and Luci Shaw. Cloth, 208 pages.

Available from your local bookstore or from Harold Shaw Publishers, Box 567, Wheaton, IL 60189. 1-800-SHAWPUB